ANNOUNCING TH
NOW IN PREPARA

The edition of *The Complete Works o*

Volume I *Behold Your King:*
      The Complete Poetical Works of Frances Ridley Havergal

Volume II *Whose I Am and Whom I Serve:*
      Prose Works of Frances Ridley Havergal

Volume III *Loving Messages for the Little Ones:*
      Works for Children by Frances Ridley Havergal

Volume IV *Love for Love: Frances Ridley Havergal:*
      Memorials, Letters and Biographical Works

Volume V *Songs of Truth and Love:*
      Music by Frances Ridley Havergal and William Henry Havergal

David L. Chalkley, Editor   Dr. Glen T. Wegge, Music Editor

The Music of Frances Ridley Havergal by Glen T. Wegge, Ph.D.

This Companion Volume to the Havergal edition is a valuable presentation of F.R.H.'s extant scores. Except for a very few of her hymn scores published in hymn-books, most or nearly all of F.R.H.'s scores have been very little—if any at all—seen, or even known of, for nearly a century. What a valuable body of music has been un-known for so long and is now made available to many. Dr. Wegge completed his Ph.D. in Music Theory at Indiana University at Bloomington, and his diligence and thoroughness in this volume are obvious. First an analysis of F.R.H.'s compositions is given, an essay that both addresses the most advanced musicians and also reach-es those who are untrained in music; then all the extant scores that have been found are newly typeset, with complete texts for each score and extensive indices at the end of the book. This volume presents F.R.H.'s music in newly typeset scores diligently prepared by Dr. Wegge, and Volume V of the Havergal edition presents the scores in facsimile, the original 19th century scores. (The essay—a dissertation—analysing her scores is given the same both in this Companion Volume and in Volume V of the Havergal edition.)

    Dr. Wegge is also preparing all of these scores for publication in performance fo-lio editions.

JESSIE'S FRIEND.

Words by F. R. H.
Music by Alberto Randegger.

For Two Voices.

Tenderly.

Little Jessie, darling pet,
    Do you want a Friend:
One who never will forget,
    Loving to the end;
One whom you can tell, when sad,
    Everything that grieves;
One who loves to make you glad;
    One who never leaves!

Such a loving Friend is ours,—
    Near us all the day;
Helping us in lesson hours,
    Smiling on our play;
Keeping us from doing wrong,
    Guarding everywhere;
Listening to each happy song,
    And each little prayer.

Jessie, if you only knew
    What He is to me,
Surely you would seek Him too,
    You would "Come and see."
Come, and you will find it true,
    Happy you will be;
Jesus says, and says to you,
    "Come! O come to Me!"

Love for Love.

1 JOHN 4:16.

KNOWING that the God on high,
  With a tender Father's grace,
Waits to hear your faintest cry,
  Waits to show a Father's face,—
Stay and think!—oh, should not you
Love this gracious Father too?

Knowing Christ was crucified,
  Knowing that He loves you now
Just as much as when He died
  With the thorns upon His brow,—
Stay and think!—oh, should not you
Love this blessèd Saviour too?

Knowing that a Spirit strives
  With your weary, wandering heart,
Who can change the restless lives,
  Pure and perfect peace impart,—
Stay and think!—oh, should not you
Love this loving Spirit too?

Frances Ridley Havergal

This next hymn was found in *God Is Love; or, Memorials of Little Nony*, a small book published in Volume IV of the Havergal edition. The author of this hymn is not known, likely not F. R. H.

I.

Lord, look upon a little child,
By nature sinful, rude, and wild;
Oh! put Thy gracious hands on me,
And make me all I ought to be.

II.

Make me Thy child, a child of God,
Washed in my Saviour's precious blood;
And my whole heart from sin set free,
A little vessel full of Thee.

III.

A star of early dawn, and bright,
Shining within Thy sacred light;
A beam of light to all around,
A little spot of hallowed ground.

IV.

Dear Jesus, take me to Thy breast,
And bless me that I may be blest;
Both when I wake and when I sleep,
Thy little lamb in safety keep.

The original book cover of Ben Brightboots, and Other True Stories, Hymns, and Music, *published by James Nisbet & Co.*

BEN BRIGHTBOOTS,

AND OTHER

True Stories, Hymns & Music.

BY

FRANCES RIDLEY HAVERGAL.

"Knowing her intense desire that Christ should be magnified, whether
by her life or in her death, may it be to His glory
that in these pages she, being dead,
'Yet speaketh ! ' "

Taken from the Edition of *The Complete Works of Frances Ridley Havergal.*

David L. Chalkley, Editor   Dr. Glen T. Wegge, Associate Editor

ISBN 978-1-937236-13-7   Library of Congress: 2011917962

Book cover by Sherry Goodwin and David Carter.

CONTENTS.

LIST OF ILLUSTRATIONS.

DEDICATION.

To F. R. H.'s Great Nephews and Nieces:

Henry Crane Lea.

John Henry Godfrey Crane.

Edith Constance Gibbons.

Rosamond Margaret Joan Gibbons.

Also to

Edward Hall Shaw.

Frances Anna Dorothea Shaw.

Agnes Sarah Georgette Shaw.

PREFATORY NOTE.

MANY loving messages reached my dear sister, F. R. H., from the readers of "Little Pillows," and "Morning Bells," entreating for another book. Gladly would she have compiled such, from the treasures of her often-told merry stories; and it was her intention to write about "Percy," as a sequel to "Bruey."

But health and time failed her, and her ever busy pen has only left these fragments.

The true story of "Ben Brightboots" was written in 1869. Her beautiful allegory "The Spirit of Beauty" shows her youthful power in composition.

"Robin Redbreast and Brown Mousie," and two or three other papers, were written for the Children's Special Service Mission, and have been translated into many languages.

The unpublished "Talk with Philip the Boatman" was written January 24th, 1879. Its deeply precious teaching reflects the sunset glow of her own life.

May these pages bring true sunshine to every reader, and new praises to our Saviour King.

MARIA V. G. HAVERGAL.

Nov. 15th, 1882.

P. S.—Will the little friends of F. R. H. accept the lines which she wrote for *my* birthday as expressive of my wishes for *theirs*.

THE blessing of the trusting one,
　　Who knows her faithful Friend;
The blessing of the waiting one,
　　Who trusts Him to the end;
The blessing of the watching one
　　Whose eyes are on the Lord;
The blessing of the chastened one,
　　That marvellous reward!
These sweetest birthday blessings be
　　Abundantly bestowed on thee!

DEAREST MARIE,—Ever so much love. I enclose you birthday wishes.

F. R. H.

Nov. 15th, 1877.

BEN BRIGHTBOOTS.

A CAT STORY.

BY THE LATE

FRANCES RIDLEY HAVERGAL.

The title page of the manuscript of "Ben Brightboots" written in F.R.H.'s handwriting.

F.R.H.'s handwritten list of chapters at the front of her manuscript of Ben Brightboots.

BEN BRIGHTBOOTS.

CHAPTER I.

KITTY.

THREE little children, named Francie, Alfred, and Alice, had a pet tabby cat. She was quite small and very playful when she first came to live with them, and they called her Kitty, a name which suited her very well at that age. There could be no mistake as to what the kitten's name was, for it was "Kitty, Kitty!" all day long, Kitty out of doors, and Kitty indoors, from the first thing in the morning to the last thing at night.

One day their eldest brother came to help them play with Kitty. He took her on his knees, and took off his watch and chain, and put it round her neck. Then he made her sit up to be admired. Francie and Alfred and Alice cut capers, and shouted, "Kitty has got brother John's watch on!"

Kitty did not altogether like being held so very carefully in brother John's hands. And she did not quite know what to make of her grand decoration. It was certainly nothing to eat, and she was not quite sure whether it was meant to be played with. She shook her little head, but that did not shake it off, because the chain was twisted round her neck. Then she began to paw it, and that made it swing about as she touched it with first one little grey paw and then the other. At this Francie and Alfred danced and shouted again, and Alice knelt on the grass by brother John's knee to watch her more closely. At last Kitty seemed to decide that the watch was a curious new plaything which she could not yet entirely understand, but which might be quite as good fun as an empty reel, if she could only get it off her neck and roll it about. But this could not be done where she was; so all at once, without any warning, she sprang through brother John's fingers, and scampered away, watch and chain and all.

Away raced Francie and Alfred and Alice after her, and brother John too, for he knew his poor watch was not very safe where it was, and if it were broken he would get more laughter than pity for it. Kitty was very knowing, and quite saw the fun of keeping the watch all to herself now she had it. It was not the first long chase there had been after her when she did not care to be caught, so she knew pretty well what bushes in the shrubbery were just too thick for the children to push through, and what short cuts there were which she could take and they could not. At other times she seemed to be quite aware that her little owners had promised not to trample on the flower beds, and considered the middle of one of them safe enough; but this time she did not try them as a refuge at all, just as if she knew that brother John was under no promise about them, and would catch her anywhere he could, even among the geraniums.

Poor little Kitty! It was four against one, and one of the four had long legs and could run very fast, while she had her heavy new plaything round her neck, and could not run quite so fast as usual.

"I've got her!" cried Alfred, from under a lilac bush.

But just as John cried out, "That's right, you're a firstrate boy!" out darted Miss Kitty, no nearer being caught than before, for he had only caught her by the tail, and that slipped through his hand like an eel. Out of the bushes, and right across the flower bed, and along the gravel path scampered Kitty, and Francie and Alice after her. Well done, Kitty! Up the knotted, twisted trunk of the large old[1] cedar tree, along a great bough nicely out of reach, and on to a little branch too weak even for Alfred's light weight, and just too high for brother John's highest jump! That was cleverly done. Kitty always knew what she was about, and she knew as well as possible that they could not reach her there. So she sat down quite comfortably and demurely, and not the least out of breath, looking most patronizingly down upon them all; while the watchglass shone brilliantly in the sunshine as it swung from her neck. It was something that it was not broken yet, as far as they could see. But brother John would much rather have had it in his pocket than have it dazzling his eyes up there. What was to be done? Alfred climbed the tree and got as far as the fork of the cedar's great bough, but it was plain that he could not get any farther without risk of a crash and "Down comes Alfred, Kitty and all!" Brother John jumped, but he might have jumped till the grass was worn out and his shoes too, before he could touch even the lowest twig of the branch on which Kitty sat in state. Alice wanted to have a ladder fetched, but there was nothing to rest it on, so that was no use. So she tried persuasion.

---

[1] [See page 74 of this book. That was the frontispiece of the original Nisbet edition of this book.]

"Kitty darling, come down. Kitty, Kitty, Kitty! Kit, Kit, Kit! Jump Kitty! Come, Kitty, Kit, the darling, the beauty, come then!"

All of which Kitty calmly listened to, and no doubt quite understood. But she was not going to be coaxed down, oh dear no! Not on any account.

Then a bright thought struck Francie.

"Alice, we'll get some milk, and entice her."

So off they ran, and very soon a nice saucer of milk was set under the tree, and the entreaties were renewed.

"Kitty dear, here's nice milk. Do come down. Kitty, Kitty, Kitty!"

Kitty eyed it. No, thank you! She was quite willing to wait till tea-time under the circumstances.

"I'll tell you what," said brother John; "it's no use watching her. She doesn't mean to come down, that's plain. We had better all come away out of sight, and then she'll get down, very likely."

So they all trooped off as if they did not care at all about Miss Kitty's proceedings. But they posted themselves just inside the hall door, from which they could see the cedar, and kept watch. It seemed a long time to wait, but brother John said it was not more than five minutes, though he had no watch to prove it, when Kitty was seen slowly creeping along the branch towards the trunk. Then they lost sight of her among the thick boughs. Presently she came in sight again, creeping and clinging down the trunk, and then with a great jump she alighted on the ground, and ran to the saucer.

"Now for it!" said brother John. "Alfred, you go round the walk behind the cedar, and get between her and the cedar. Alice, you go behind the laurels, and be ready to catch her if she runs that way. Francie, you go that side, and I'll go this, and then she *will* be sharp if she gets off again."

So they all crept softly to their appointed places, while Kitty lapped up the milk, with the watch dangling in the saucer. Brother John came quickly behind her, pounced upon her, and had her safe; not by the tail, like Alfred.

Now for the watch. It really was not much the worse, for except a crack across the glass no harm seemed to be done. John told the children that its bath in the milk would not have hurt it, and that a new glass would only cost sixpence, and he thought they had had sixpennyworth of fun. They were very glad to hear it, and would not have minded tying the watch on again, but brother John had had enough of that sort of fun, and was not very likely to tie his watch round any more kittens' necks.

CHAPTER II.

MOTHER AND BEN.

After a while Kitty grew up out of kittenhood, and became a very sedate and well behaved cat. When at last she had three little kittens of her own it did not seem at all right and proper to call her Kitty any longer, so by general consent she was called "Mother," as being much more suitable and dignified. It came to be known to the three little cat keepers that Grandpapa Havergal would very much like to have a kitten, if one could be found pretty enough, and well behaved enough, for the great honour of going to live with him at Leamington. Great consultations were held on the subject. Mother must not be sent, that was soon settled; for she was too old to be likely to learn to love grandpapa to the degree which a cat of proper feelings would be expected to do. And she might even run away from her new home if she were taken from her old one at Winterdyne, where she had watched so many sparrows and caught so many mice. Besides, Mother was their own, own pussy, and it would be very hard to part with her, even for grandpapa. So the choice lay between Mother's three children. One was a tabby like herself, another was black, and the third was black with a little white. Everybody was asked which was the prettiest, and everybody said the same. There never was a prettier kitten than the little black fellow with four white paws and a little white waistcoat. He was a sturdy little kitten too, and opened his eyes a whole day before his sisters, and could mew the loudest of the three, and, better still, could purr the loudest. And Alice said he was the first who found his way out of the basket in which they lived, and made a voyage of discovery all across the servants' hall on his own account. So it was settled that he was to be grandpapa's kitten as soon as he was old enough to be sent away from Mother.

Next came the grand question of finding a name for him. For about a week every one who came to the house was asked whether they knew any *very* pretty name for a cat. Whereupon every one mentioned the names of any cats with which they happened to be personally acquainted, which were not always very pretty, and often the same over again.

"What a number of Kitties and Tabbies and Toms there are in the world!" said Francie. "If I were a pussy I would almost rather be called 'Smut,' like old Mrs. Morris's cat, than have just the same name as so many others."

Names for the other two kittens were easily found. Jetty and Tabby did very well for them. But could nobody find a name that sounded right for grandpapa's kitten? "Let us write and ask grandpapa himself," said Francie. "Then he will be sure to like it, and it would be such a pity if we chose a name he did not like." So the lines were ruled, and a letter was written containing a full, true, and particular description of grandpapa's kitten elect.

Grandpapa answered by return of post, for he knew how the postbag would be watched for till his answer came. "Call him Ben," said the letter, "and ask auntie to tell you why. If he must have a surname, let him be Ben Brightboots."

"*Ben Brightboots.*" That was exactly what they wanted. "Ben" was a nice short name to call him by, and "Brightboots" made a difference between him and all the other Bens in the world. There was no fear of his ever meeting a namesake. And surely no other Ben had such pretty little white feet, so it was quite right he should have such a compliment paid to them.

Alfred was sent to fetch Ben, that he might be taught his new name, and that papa and mamma might see how well it did for him. And if he did not learn to know it in the next half hour it was not the fault of his teachers, for it was "Ben! Ben! Ben!" from first one and then another, and then from all three at once, till the poor little fellow must have wondered what all the noise was about.

At last Francie remembered that they had not yet heard from Aunt Fanny why grandpapa chose this name, so Ben was carried back to Mother, who made a funny little loving noise when she saw him, and welcomed him back to the basket with a good licking all over his little black coat and white waistcoat.

CHAPTER III.

BEN THE FIRST AND CANON BEN.

"Auntie, we have got a letter from grandpapa. And he says we are to call his kitten Ben Brightboots, and that you will tell us why."

And Francie, who had charge of the letter because she was the eldest, unfolded it very carefully and gave it to auntie to read. When auntie had read it she said: "I will tell you all about it. It is because grandpapa had a beautiful cat several years ago which was called Ben, and so he would like to have another of the same name. 'Ben the First' was quite black, with very large fierce eyes, which must have frightened all the rats and mice most terribly. He was a very queer tempered individual. Nothing ever seemed to disturb him; he was too proud and grave to hiss or spit or scratch, but if any one offended him he would get up very slowly, glare at them with his splendid great eyes, and walk solemnly away. No one ever made friends with him. Once a lady came who always won the heart of every cat and kitten she had to do with, and she tried her very best to win my lord Ben. She petted and coaxed him and talked to him; she practised various ways of stroking his head and fingering his ears and cheeks which had never been known to fail with any other cat; she gave him the nicest bits of meat, and fetched saucers of milk at times when he had no right to expect a drop. It was all in vain. He ate the meat and lapped the milk in a most ungrateful way, never arching his head or raising his tail by way of saying thank you. He endured her petting and nursing just as long as she held him and no longer, jumping heavily down from her knee the moment she loosed him, and walking away under the table, as if he meant to show that he wished to have nothing to do with her. Never a purr could she get from him with all her kindness and pains, nothing but sulky silence. He did not even condescend to scratch her, but behaved altogether as if she were not worthy to be taken any notice of, good or bad. He would sometimes look up if she called him, but looked away again directly, as much as to say, 'Oh, it's only you, is it? I would not have looked if I had known.' As for coming when called, it never occurred to him to do such a thing. He cared for nobody, and so of course nobody cared for him, and we all thought him a very unloveable cat. Yet after all he was a very affectionate cat in his way. There now, Alice! how could that be? He had given so much love to grandpapa that he had none to spare for any one else. That is quite different from you, is it not? For I think the more love you give to dear grandpapa, the more you will have to spare for other people. It is very nice to love everybody, and makes us much happier than loving only one or two. I know two little girls and a little boy who have a great many to love and a great many who love them. And I think these little children ought to be very glad of this, and very thankful to the One who loves them best of all, for giving them so many to love. Don't you think so, Francie?"

Francie's answer was a kiss which meant "Yes!" and Alfred said the same in a way of his own, which was a grunt sounding more like "No!" but auntie knew it meant "Yes" all the same. And Alice said, "Ducky darling auntie!" which was only another way of saying the same thing.

"Did Ben the First really love grandpapa?" asked Alfred.

"I really think he did," said auntie. "For he never seemed happy anywhere away from him; and if he was shut out of his study he would sit patiently at the door with his great eyes shining in the dark passage till the door was opened, and then he would walk gravely in, and sit down close by his feet, or even on them if he could, and never move till his master went away. When grandpapa went away from home he sulked and moped more than ever, and would have nothing to do with any one. When he came back he would brighten up and seem quite cheerful, and follow him all over the house, walk slowly round and round his legs when he stood still, and sit down on his feet as soon as he sat down.

"He was always the same, paying constant attention to his master, and never taking the least notice of any one else.

"At last one winter we missed him suddenly, and felt sure something must be wrong, for he was too sober a cat to have gone holiday-making on his own account, especially when his master was at home. Day after day went on, and we could hear nothing of him. One morning a little boy came to the Vicarage and said, 'Please, sir, your cat's been killed. Robinson's dog killed her in a minute.'

"This was very sad news, not that we loved poor Ben for his own sake, but we cared for anything that loved grandpapa.

"Then we had another pussy, and called him Ben in memory of the other. He was black too, and very handsome indeed, with a magnificent tail. But he had a little white at his throat which looked like a little pair of bands. So we called him 'Canon Ben.'

"Soon after he received this title, grandpapa went away from home for a long time, and Uncle Frank said he would take Canon Ben home to his cloister rooms by the cathedral, lest he should be neglected or lost while we were all away. We were very glad of this, for he was a nice amiable cat, and made friends with us all, and purred when he was pleased, which Ben the First never condescended to do at all. So he went away to his new quarters which suited his name exactly. He soon became a well known character, was on excellent terms with the minor canons, and quite intimate with the bishop. He was never quite sure about the chorister boys, and kept them at a respectful distance.

"His favourite seat on sunny afternoons was on a wall overlooking the garden of the bishop's palace. Perhaps the bishop reminded him of his old master, for if he caught sight of him he would come down from the wall, walk round him, and rub against his legs, and arch his back and tail as a token of his wish to be very friendly, and then go back to his perch and watch him till he went in. He was a very peaceably disposed cat, and we never heard of his picking any quarrels with any of the other cats which lived in the cloisters and belonged to other minor canons. Canon Ben kept himself to himself, and cared for no company but the bishop and clergy.

"But there was one inhabitant of the cloisters who interfered considerably with Ben's peace and comfort, and would not let him lead the quiet life to which he was inclined. This was a large grey parrot who lived on the opposite side of the green square round which the cloisters ran. On fine days Polly's cage was hung among the ivy in the cloister arch before her master's door. No doubt Polly thought this arrangement an excellent one, for she could see all that went on, and could make remarks to every one who came to pay a call at any door in the cloisters. And strangers were sometimes very much astonished to hear a voice screaming to them all across the square, 'Rub your shoes! Fine day, sir! Very well, thank you! Rub your shoes!' Polly never missed an opportunity of teasing Canon Ben, and he never crossed the square without receiving a salutation of some kind. No one was told so often to rub his shoes as he, and he might have got used to rude speeches of that kind, but Polly was always finding new ways of annoying him. Sometimes she would mew like two or three cats at once, and when he came nearer to see whether he had any fellow pussies in distress she would begin yelping like a very little puppy. Sometimes she would give a soft musical whistle just like Uncle Frank's, and when he obeyed it like a dutiful cat as he was, and looked about for his master, she would squeal like a pig, or say, 'Mind your business!'

"Canon Ben seemed to bear it patiently for some time, but I am afraid he was planning revenge in his heart. One hot August afternoon, when everything was as still as night, when everybody who could was keeping indoors because of the great heat, when all the cats and dogs in the town were having an after-dinner doze, and even Polly was quite sleepy and had not made a single remark for two hours, Uncle Frank happened to look out of his little ivy-arched window on the shady side of the green square, and saw Canon Ben creeping very slowly close under the wall towards Polly's cage. He meant mischief, that was plain, or he would not have gone in that stealthy way, crouching under the ivy, now and then stretching up his head and then lowering it, but always keeping his eyes fixed on Polly, who sat half asleep on her perch and facing the other way. On he came till he was close to the arch, which was like a large window with no glass in it; and then he crouched like a little tiger for a spring on the stone sill just above which the cage hung.

"Perhaps Polly heard the rustle of an ivy leaf, for all at once she turned round and saw how the land lay. In an instant she shouted 'Who are you?' so suddenly and fiercely that Ben stopped, and looked quite startled. 'Who are you?' pealed again like a very squeaky trumpet through the cloisters. Ben was not prepared with an answer, and still did not spring.

"'Bow, wow, wow, wow, wow, wow! Bow! Wow! Wow! Bow, wow, wow, wow, wow, wow, wow!' stormed Polly, barking savagely and loudly enough to wake all the dogs in Hereford, not to mention cats.

"Ben showed signs of retreating. Accustomed as he was to Polly's ways, he could not quite stand this. Polly saw his weakness and kept it up. 'Bow, wow, wow, wow, wow!' There might have been a whole kennel of dogs behind her. Ben quailed and quivered, and quickly turned tail and fled, never stopping till he was safe on the high wall over the bishop's garden, where he knew no dogs could reach him. Polly was so proud of her victory that no one had a chance of a nap for the rest of that afternoon, and though no errand boys and no visitors came, nor any more cats, and she had it all to herself, she sang and talked and whistled and barked till the sun went down behind the cloister roof, and her arch was left shady and cool. It was a year before grandpapa was at home again, and long before that time Canon Ben had become so established at Hereford that it was thought a pity to take him away from Uncle Frank.

"So grandpapa has been for a long time without any pussy to love him, and I am very glad you are going to send Ben Brightboots to him."

"How soon can he go, auntie?" asked Alfred.

"If we asked Mother about it," replied auntie, "she would say, 'I can't spare my little son yet. He must learn to pick bones first; and he ought to have at least a lesson or two in catching mice before he goes away. I think it is right to bring up my kittens so that they can get their own living if it should be necessary. One never knows what may happen.'"

"He can't go till somebody takes him," said Francie. "He wouldn't be passenger, and he wouldn't be goods, so he will have to wait till grandpapa comes again to fetch him."

Alice thought that would be a good plan, because it might make grandpapa come a little sooner, and it might make Ben's departure a little later, both of which would be very desirable arrangements.

CHAPTER IV.

A TERRIBLE CALAMITY.

Poor little Mother did not know what a terrible calamity was going to fall on her family. She had been so happy in keeping all her children, instead of having them taken away to be drowned, that she must have thought all the dangers of their infancy were over. Ben had been saved for grandpapa, Jetty for Mrs. Turner the gatekeeper, and Tabby was to be daughter at home, and to be brought up at Winterdyne, as the house was quite large enough to accommodate two cats. But one dark night, when the kittens were about three weeks old, Mother, who had sat in her basket with them all day long, went out for a short airing. Perhaps she had a private idea that she might bring back their first mouse, as she had been too busy with her nursery duties to catch any before that time.

When she came back there was no Tabby in the basket, and Ben and Jetty were mewing loudly; they had been crying for Mother, poor little things, with all their might. And no wonder, for a great black rat had watched his opportunity, and carried off little sister Tabby without heeding their cries. And by the time Mother reached home little Tabby was eaten up, all but some little bits of soft fur, which remained to show what the cruel rat had done.

Mother comforted Ben and Jetty, talked to them in her own way, and licked them; so they soon left off mewing, for they knew they were safe with her, and that the naughty rat would not dare to come again while she was there with her sharp claws and teeth ready to catch him and eat him up in his turn as he deserved.

Ben and Jetty soon went to sleep, but Mother had other things to think about. She made up her mind what to do before the sun rose, or any one was moving in the house. It would never do to stay there any longer. The basket was very comfortable, and the hay was very soft; but the rat knew the way to it, and it was of more consequence to be safe than comfortable.

When Louisa the dairymaid came downstairs she went to look at the kittens before beginning her work, for she was very fond of them and very kind to Mother in saving little bits and scraps for her. But the basket was empty, the hay was all scuffled about, and neither Mother nor Ben nor Jetty were anywhere to be seen. They had left no message to say when they would be at home, nor where they were gone. Poor Francie and Alfred and Alice! It was very hard to pay attention to subtraction and spelling that morning, and even the English history did not seem so interesting as usual. It had nothing to do with cats, or rats either, and what did they care about kings and queens in comparison?

After lessons there was a grand hunt for the lost family. Every likely and unlikely place was searched, cellars and offices, and washhouse and coachhouse, and haylofts and sheds, but all in vain. Mother was too clever for the seekers, and her hiding place was never found at all, which was a sore disappointment. After this she came every day like a little beggar for milk and bones, but always managed to get away again without betraying her secret. It was no use watching her, for she never went the same way twice; and if any one followed her she always contrived to disappear among the bushes, where even Alfred could not keep up with her.

"Never mind," said mamma. "Depend upon it, Ben and Jetty are all safe, and when they are old enough to run about they will find their way to the house again. Mother would not stay away if they were dead, she would come back and live in the house as she used to do. Only wait a few weeks and you will see." A few weeks might not seem much to mamma, but it seemed a very long time to the children. Still it was something to have a fair hope of seeing the kittens again at last.

The leaves were falling one cold wet autumn day, and Francie and Alfred and Alice could only watch them through the window instead of going out to play among them. A tap was heard at the schoolroom door, and Francie said "Come in!" The door opened, and who should come in but Louisa with a pretty kitten in her apron!

"It's Ben Brightboots! it's dear Ben, grandpapa's Ben!" they shouted. And then there was such a dancing and shouting and capering and chattering, that one would have thought it must have taken about fifteen boys to make the amount of noise, instead of one boy and two little girls.

"Oh, Louisa, where did you find him? the darling!" cried Alice, as soon as they had let off some of the steam. Louisa told them that she found him in one of the garden walks under the beech trees, looking very dismal and rather wet. Then there was a general scampering all over the house, till every one in it had been found, and called upon to admire Master Ben, and to look how much he had grown, and how pretty his whiskers were, and twenty other things. Jetty was hardly thought of; it was enough for one day to have Ben home again. It was the first time there had been such great rejoicings over Ben Brightboots, but it was not to be the last. And when brother Willie came home from school there was another rejoicing over Ben.

CHAPTER V.

A JOURNEY AND A NEW HOME

Weeks went on, and the days grew shorter, and Ben Brightboots grew larger and prettier. As for growing more playful, that was hardly possible, for he was always at play unless he was asleep. He evidently thought it the great business of his life. He was right, for it made his little body grow stronger and more agile, and so it was the same use to him that books and lessons were to his little master and mistresses, who had minds as well as bodies, and needed something to make these stronger and cleverer.

He held the further opinion that everything in the house was meant for a toy, especially every small thing which could be rolled about. Sofas and chairs were certainly intended for his especial entertainment, for he could roll reels of cotton round and round the legs, and practise jumping through or over the backs; besides which, if he sat on the top of the sofa, he could see all over the room at once, and pounce down upon anything that caught his eye. Now and then he took a quieter mood, and then he was very loving and grateful, and had a pretty way of lifting up his little fore feet, and pawing with them, something like a beautiful spirited horse, only more gracefully and less impatiently.

Christmas was near, and Aunt Fanny was going home to grandpapa. So this would be a good escort for Ben, and the children made their minds up that it would be selfish to keep him any longer, now that he was quite old enough to leave Mother.

When the morning came for his journey, all the baskets in the house, big and little, were brought together, to see which would do best for a travelling carriage. It was very well meant, but mamma said the children might have made their heads save their heels, and not have brought baskets large enough for half a dozen cats, and baskets which would not have held a rat. But they were very willing to carry them all away again, after one had been chosen just large enough for Ben to lie down in, with a lid to it. Some nice dry hay was fetched and put into it, and then it was set on the hearth rug wide open, and Ben was sent for.

When he came he did exactly what they hoped he would do, knowing how inquisitive he always was. He walked straight up to the basket, and nearly overset it to begin with. Then he began to paw the handle, and to play with a bit of hay which hung over the side. Then he stood on his hind legs, put his fore paws on the edge and looked in. Then he drew back, gave a little spring, and in he went! Out again, with a bit of hay in his mouth, and then in again, this time upsetting the basket, which frightened him away for a minute, but he soon came back again. Francie and Alfred and Alice watched him all the time, but did not interfere with him, except to set the basket up again. He was getting accustomed to his travelling carriage so nicely that it was better to let him alone.

"Next time he gets in," said Francie, "we will shut the lid down, for it is nearly time for auntie to start."

After a little more play, Ben got into the basket once more and lay down, and then Francie and Alfred and Alice all ran up and stroked him, and put their little faces down into the basket to give him a good-bye kiss, and then mamma said they had really better shut the lid down at once, for the carriage was just coming round to the door. A nice little bit of meat was given him as a parting present, and then the basket was closed and tied with a piece of string.

They could still see him through the wickerwork. He was quite happy, and seemed to think that having the lid shut down made his bed all the more cosy. Alice cried out: "Oh what a good contented puss he is; he has begun to purr quite loud! Just listen, Francie." And he went on purring up to the very last. Perhaps he heard Francie and Alfred and Alice shouting after the carriage: "Good-bye, Ben Brightboots! Be a good Ben to grandpapa, and love him! Good-bye, Ben darling!" But as he did not know what "Good-bye" meant, it did not make him at all low spirited, and soon after the train had started auntie peeped in, and found he was fast asleep.

It was not a very long journey, and yet auntie and Ben had to change trains, and wait half an hour at Birmingham. She carried him into the warm waiting room, and shut the door, for she was afraid he might be frightened, and dash out of the basket and try to run away when he found himself in such a strange place. She set the basket on the table, and opened it very carefully. There was Ben Brightboots, wide-awake, and looking up at her with his bright, pretty eyes, but lying as comfortably as if he had never slept anywhere else in his life, and purring so that you could have heard him all across the room except when the engines rumbled and squealed. He was quite too comfortable to think of moving at all, much less of running away. That evidently never occurred to him.

Little Alice had put some little bits of meat in paper, and given them to auntie for Ben's lunch so she took them out of her bag and gave them to him one by one. He ate them slowly, in a very gentlemanly way, without any snatching or gobbling. It was very well behaved of him, but might be accounted for by the fact that it was the second lunch he had had that morning.

When the new home was reached grandpapa himself opened the basket. He did not lift Ben out, but let him get out himself, just as he got in. But he stroked him and talked to him in such a way that Ben soon made up his mind to be on good terms. He got out, and stood on the table, and gave himself a good stretch. But then he began to look about him, and in spite of grandpapa's welcome he did not much like seeing nothing but strange things round him. He jumped from the table and ran under it, and sat down, looking unhappy, and puzzled as to what it could all mean. "Wait a bit," said grandpapa, "give him time. He will soon be at home. Leave him to me." Presently he crept out, and came to the hearthrug, holding up one little white foot as if he were not sure where it would be safe to set it down next. Then grandpapa stooped, and picked him up very gently, and sat down in the arm chair, making a very comfortable nest for him inside his coat. He stroked his head and twisted his ears, and rubbed his fingers behind them, in a way which Ben appeared to think very nice and kind, for he did not try to run away but actually began to purr. And before night Ben had become quite resigned and cheerful, and even played with grandpapa's handkerchief, and with an empty reel which grannie found for him.

It would make the story quite too long if all Ben's doings in the next few weeks were faithfully recorded. Of all the Toms and Tabbies, and Kitties and Katties, and Bens too that grandpapa ever had, Ben Brightboots was the greatest favourite. Never was there a half grown kitten so pretty and playful and affectionate and funny as he; and never was any cat, not even Ben the First, more devoted to grandpapa. He would follow him about everywhere, and never seem so contented as when he could sit on grandpapa's knee. Sometimes he was not thinking about the cat, and leant back in his chair with his legs stretched out, so that there was no comfortable lap for him. And then Ben would try over and over again to make a seat on them, slipping down every minute and climbing up again, till at last grandpapa would say, "Poor little fellow!" and draw in his feet and make a cosy place for him under his coat.

At first grannie made a rule that Ben was never to go upstairs; but when, in spite of this, he found his way up to grandpapa's study, and would persist in sitting on his desk to help him write his sermons and letters, purring out all the love in his little heart, and getting up now and then to rub affectionately against his head and shoulder, what was to be done! Grannie could not find it in her heart to enforce the rule, so far as the study was concerned. But she said it must be kept as to the bedrooms; Ben must not go there. But even in this Ben was too much for her, as we shall see in the next chapter.

It really seemed as if he had set himself to win grannie's heart, and make up for his defiance of this one rule. He never did anything else which he ought not to do; never came in with wet and dirty feet, never stole anything from the pantry, never even in his wildest gambols did any mischief. Not but what he did sometimes jump on the tables and sideboard, and touch everything with his little soft paw to see whether it would move, and whether it was meant to play with. But he never knocked anything down, and though these little voyages of discovery were watched rather anxiously, he moved so gently and gracefully and looked so happy and good tempered that he was allowed to do pretty much what he liked.

After all grannie's declarations that cats ought to be kept in their proper place, and not come into parlours at all, Ben might have been seen any evening of that Christmas time, not only in the parlour, but sitting triumphantly on grannie herself as she lay on her sofa at work, and catching her thread as it passed in and out, as if she were using her needle for nothing else in the world but his amusement. Especially if she had anything in the way of ribbon or lace did he make a point of persecuting her, unrolling the ribbon, and clawing the lace, and pretending to be very busy with it, once even going the length of lying down and rolling upon it. Then grannie would look up and say: "What am I to do? This cat won't let me work, it is of no use to try. Ben, why don't you go to your master? I don't want you, I'm sure."

And all the while grannie was as pleased as any one to watch his funny little ways, and quite enjoyed being interrupted, and liked him all the better for his pretty impudence.

Ben was quite a little gentleman in his manners. Mother had taught him how to wash himself and keep his fur nice, and he did it as carefully as if she were watching him all the time, so that the white waistcoat and white boots were always beautifully clean. He was extremely particular about his whiskers, which were very long and handsome, and could not bear to let them touch anything he was eating. If grandpapa gave him his porridge cup to finish, he would not put his head into it; he would only lick round the edges and eat any little bits which he could reach without soiling his whiskers, though if a bit of porridge were given him in a saucer or plate he would eat it up without any daintiness.

Sometimes Ben had a sort of game of hide and seek by himself. He had a plaything of his own, a little ball which he rolled about and darted after, and caught up in his fore paws and sat up with it like a little squirrel. In the evening when the curtains were drawn he sometimes gave it such a push that it rolled under them, and he could not find it without having quite a hunt for it, and sometimes it really seemed as if he had pretended to lose it for the fun of pretending to find it again.

He found a great deal to learn in his new home, and he was always learning something in his own fashion. Not a cupboard or a drawer could be opened but he must go and see what was in it, and watch everything that was done till it was shut again. He was especially curious about the washing up of the tea things, sitting on the dresser and taking note of what was done with every cup and saucer. One evening it occurred to him that he had never yet fully understood the mysteries of the dining room lamp. So he sprang on the table, and walked deliberately up to it and two or three times round it. Then he pawed the lower part all round. Then he touched the little handle by which it was wound up. Then he tried the screw which raised or lowered the wick. Next he stretched up his neck and took the edge of the shade in his mouth. It was not good to eat, but he tried it at two or three other places, till he was quite sure of the fact. Then he put his head under it, and looked close at the light, till the pupils of his eyes shrank up to a mere little line of black. Finally he put his nose close to the glass. But he did not reckon on the glass being hot, and his poor little black nose must have suffered for his curiosity, for one touch was enough! Down he jumped, and never wanted to know any more about the lamp.

One day there had been a great deal of snow and a high wind had blown it into deep drifts. Ben knew nothing yet about snow. He did not very much like it, still he must go and see for himself what all that white stuff might be. He went out into the garden and peered about, stepping delicately along the cold paths. Presently, for some reason best known to himself, he made a tremendous spring at what looked like a firm white bank. It was a drift of fine loose snow, and in he went, quite over his head, so that for a few moments nothing could be seen of him. He scrambled out, puzzled and frightened, and looking as if he had been rolled in a flour bin. He shook off his white overcoat as well as he could, and scampered away into the house as fast as possible. He had learnt quite enough about snowdrifts, and did not care to study them any more.

CHAPTER VI.

LOST AND FOUND.

All the fun and play came to an end one day. Grandpapa was taken very ill, and went upstairs to bed, and the doctor came, and everything was very sad and gloomy.

Ben seemed to understand that something was wrong, and was perfectly miserable. He ran up and down stairs like a wild thing; when he got to the top he did not seem to know what he had come for, and tore down again. Then he would scamper up again, and run to the study, and sit on the shut desk and mew. Then he would come down again, and get into his master's arm chair in the dining room, and turn round and round in it, but not lie down. Then he went to the stairs again, and sat first on one step, and then on another, in a restless way, as if no place were comfortable to him. At last he followed grannie into grandpapa's room. Ah, she would not send him away then, poor little loving fellow! He jumped at once on to the bed, and went very softly up to grandpapa's poor hand, and licked it; and then crept down to the bottom of the bed and down on his feet, as if he meant to try and keep them warm. After that he lay there almost all day long, and never seemed to care to run about and play as he used to do. Early every morning he came up and sat and mewed outside the door till he was let in, and then as quick as lightning he was on the bed, always going up to grandpapa's head first, and fondling, and purring, and making curious little bleating noises, meant to be very kind and sympathising. It was his way of saying "Good morning, dear master, I am so glad the door is opened at last. I do hope you are better. I wish I could make you well." Then he would creep down to keep grandpapa's feet warm.

After many days and nights of pain, grandpapa began to get better and come downstairs. Ben was delighted to see him in his right place again, the arm chair by the fire, and did everything he could to show it, purring and arching his back, and setting his tail straight up, and rubbing round and round grandpapa's legs and the legs of the chair too.

Now who could help loving such a cat as Ben Brightboots? Grandpapa loved him more than ever, and so did auntie; and as for grannie, she would have let him roll over all her ribbons and eat up all her lace if he pleased, he had so completely won her heart. The servants liked him and petted him too, so he was as well off as any cat in the kingdom. But then he deserved it all, if any cat did!

One morning he did not come in to prayers as usual, and breakfast was had without him too. "Foolish fellow, not to come for his milk!" said grandpapa; "where can he be?" The bell was rung, and the servant was asked if Ben was in the kitchen. No, she had not seen him anywhere. "Very likely he is in your study," said auntie; "I'll go and see." But Ben was not there. Nor in grandpapa's bedroom, nor in any other room in the house. It might be that he had been invited to cold rat by some new acquaintance of his own kind, and would be home to dinner. But dinner time came, and no Ben; and teatime came, and no Ben; and bedtime came, and still no Ben. It was quite serious; something must have happened, for Ben would never have stayed away all day of his own free will.

Next day inquiries were made among all the neighbours, but no one had seen or heard anything of him. The day after a boy was set to work. He was to go to every house in the neighbourhood, and ask if any one had seen a very pretty young black cat with four white feet. The boy came back in the evening for the shilling, which was to have been two if he had found Ben, with nothing to tell except that "Nobody hadn't heard nothing of no black cat with four white feet."

It was gravely proposed to advertise in the papers, or at least to have him cried by the bellman, but it was decided that this would be of no use, because if he were alive and free he would surely come back of his own accord. It was more likely that he had been killed, and that no more would ever be heard of him.

Day after day went on, and hope became fainter. At last grandpapa wrote to tell Francie and Alfred and Alice of his sad loss, his pretty Ben Brightboots whom they had nursed up for him, and sent him all the way from Winterdyne, lost, perhaps dead. It was not a very cheerful breakfast after that letter came out of the post-bag. The three children went to Mother as soon as breakfast was over, and told her all about it, and stroked and petted and pitied her. At which attention Mother was much gratified, and purred as merrily as if not a word had been said and her son had been still safe in grandpapa's keeping. What a good thing it was that poor little Mother could not understand what was said, only what was done to her; and that being all kindness made her quite happy.

I am so glad that this is not the very end of the story of Ben Brightboots. It is so much nicer to have a pleasant ending than a sad one, especially when it is true, which I beg to state this little story really is, and not all make-up.

For some time grandpapa and grannie and auntie watched and hoped. Not long after Ben was lost a great mewing was heard one evening. It seemed to come from the other side of the road. But when the door was opened, and auntie called "Ben, Ben!" it suddenly stopped. Next night it was heard again, but the same thing happened. And then it was found that it was only some mischievous boys imitating a cat, perhaps because they knew of the inquiries which had been made. When this false alarm was over there seemed to be nothing to do but to give up hope. Poor dear Ben!

A whole year passed away, and never a word was heard of him. Before it was over the servants who knew him had both gone away, and new ones were come. One day Mary came to grannie, and said: "If you please ma'am, there's such a pretty cat sat on the drawing room window sill. He was mewing there at seven o'clock this morning. He came after me into the kitchen, and we gave him some milk, and then he went back again and sat on the window, and he's been there ever since."

"I thought I heard a cat mewing," said grannie. "What is he like?"

"He's nearly all black," answered Mary, "and he has white paws, and keeps on lifting them up and down."

"Fetch him in, and let me look at him," said grannie.

So Mary fetched the cat and put him down in the hall. Could it possibly be Ben? There was the black coat, and the white waistcoat, and the four pretty white boots. Only this was a full-grown cat, and when Ben went away he was not nearly full grown, but of course he would be so by this time if he were alive.

So grannie called grandpapa, and he came down, and auntie heard something going on about a cat and came too.

As soon as grandpapa appeared the cat went up to him, and began rubbing round his legs, and doing everything a cat could do to show that he was no stranger. They all went into the dining room, and said, "Let us see what the cat will do." He followed them in, and went on rubbing round grandpapa, now and then turning away to rub against grannie's and auntie's dresses, walking from one to the other as if he were quite at home, and knew the room and the persons quite well. "It must be Ben," said auntie. "It can't be Ben," said grannie. "I never in all my life heard or read of a cat remembering in this way for such a length of time," said grandpapa; "and yet I do believe it is Ben. See, he does just as Ben used to do."

He sat down in the arm chair. Up jumped the cat, and sat on his knee, lifting up first one little paw and then the other. "Look, look!" said auntie: "that proves it must be Ben. That is exactly how he always lifted up his little feet, and I never saw any other cat do it in just the same way."

Then grandpapa got up, and went upstairs. The cat followed him, and when they reached the top it darted on before, and ran straight to grandpapa's room, passing all the other doors. Was it likely a strange cat would have done that? "But," said grannie, "is it likely that a cat could remember everything for a whole year?" Certainly not, for cats have not generally very good memories. But it was still less likely that a strange cat would be so very affectionate to the right person all at once, and know its way about the house, and do every single thing just as Ben used to do, and seem so very much delighted with everybody and everything, besides having the white boots and white waistcoat, which could not have been begged, borrowed, or stolen. So at last they all gave up saying "It must be Ben," and said "It *is* Ben."

Ben was so happy that he hardly sat down all that day, but kept walking about, fondling every one and expecting to be fondled in return.

"Pretty Ben!" said grannie; "you want to tell us where you have been all this time. Speak to us, Ben! Were they kind to you, Ben?"

It was a comfort that his good looks answered that question. Wherever he had been he must have been well treated, for he was plump and strong, and his fur was beautifully smooth and glossy. He had not been starved at any rate.

Mary was told that if any one came to inquire after him they were to be asked in, so that an explanation might be given. But no one ever came, so grandpapa was left in peaceable possession of his cat.

A letter was written to Winterdyne to announce this happy return. It was addressed to "Miss Frances Shaw & Co."

"Pyrmont Villa, Leamington.

My Darlings:

"'Ding, dong, bome, bell!
Poor pussy safe and well!'

"Our pretty Ben Brightboots is actually come back again! This morning early our new servant saw a pretty black and white-footed cat sitting outside the drawing room window. He followed her to the kitchen, and then returned to the window. Nothing was said till after breakfast, when the servant remarked to grandmamma how singular it was that a pretty cat should come into the house. Grandmamma sent for him, and lo, it was *Ben!* I was soon called. He directly knew me, came to me, and let me fondle him. He is in good condition, and must have been taken care of by somebody. He is quite at home, and plays and goes about just as he did a full year ago. It is really a wonderful circumstance; I do not know that I ever heard the like, so I lose no time in telling you about it. I am sure you will all be glad at the restoration.

"Poor Ben! he cannot tell us what has happened to him nor where he has been. And, dear ones, many a poor little black slave-boy has been brought back to father or mother without being able to tell his absent history. Not so when we, like black sheep, 'are returned to the Shepherd of souls.' He knows all about us, and helps us too to tell Him all. Thus little silent Ben may teach us a speaking lesson. Our love to you all. I am sure Ben would join if he knew how.

"Ever your affectionate

"Grandpapa Havergal."

When the letter came Francie opened it, while Alfred and Alice looked over. Francie read as far as the words, "Ben Brightboots is actually come back again!" and then it might have been a room full of wild Indians for the screaming and shouting! Alice did not wait to hear the rest, but raced away to the top of the house, where Louisa was ill in bed, to tell her the wonderful news. And in less than five minutes, thanks to Francie's and Alfred's legs and lungs, every one else in the house was made aware of it. And how they wished that brother Willie was not at school. Mother was duly informed of the fact, and purred very properly, though she could not have been much the wiser for the information. It seemed quite a pity that she could not enter into all the rejoicing; but as she had not shared the sorrow when her son was lost, this only made it equal, which is the case in many much more important concerns.

This is a story without an end, for Ben has not yet come to an end; and as he is still young and not at all above having a game of play, it is to be hoped that he will live till Francie and Alfred and Alice and all the other little boys and girls who may read about him are grown up and have done with story books.

It does not seem likely that it will ever be found out what became of him all that year. He will not be so easily lost again, for he now wears a little collar of scarlet leather with grandpapa's name and address on it. Next time Francie and Alfred and Alice come to Leamington we shall see whether Ben's wonderful memory is long enough to remember them. I should not be surprised if it is. How pleased they will be!

[*More news about Ben.*]

"*Pyrmont Villa, February* 12*th.*

"My dear Alice:

"Aunt Maria must tell you all about pretty Ben, all about his little pranks and frolics and his fond doings with me, *just* as before he travelled from us. Happily the servants are very fond of him. So you may be glad I did not bring away the other kitten from Winterdyne which you had ready for me.

"Thus it is in *far* greater matters the Creator of cats, who is the Redeemer of our souls, arranges for all who love Him, because He often brings it to pass that what we *much* wish for at one time we soon after dislike or refuse. So learn, dear Alice, always to be moderate and content. Love to each one around.

"Ever affectionately yours,

"Grandpapa W. H. Havergal."

The following lines were written by an elderly gentleman who witnessed the scene described in Chapter I.

Dear brother John was so much smitten
With our right frisky little kitten,
That he, in playfulness, would train
Pussy to wear a watch and chain!
No sooner thought of than 'twas done:
Puss hardly comprehends the fun;

But, scampering off in foolish fright,
Tried to escape with all her might,
Breaking the watch in her wild race
Ere we could check her headlong pace.
From this exploit we take for granted
That not for cats are watches wanted!

ALEXANDER PARKER.

WINTERDYNE, July 10th, 1869.

The Cedar Tree of Winterdyne.

"They shall perish; but Thou remainest."
(Psalm 102:26, P. B.V.)   [Prayer Book Version]

O CEDAR tree of Winterdyne,
    The shading guardian of our peaceful home,
        How much we all loved thee!
Thy boughs in summer seemed to cool the air
For those who sat beneath. In wintry frost and snow
A hoary sire thou seem'dst. In stormy winds
We loved to see how bravely thou didst stand,
        Nor thought that *thou* couldst fall.

O Cedar tree of Winterdyne,
    How many a tale thou could'st have told
        Of festive pleasant times—
But pass we by the gathering throngs
From far and near with gladsome songs,
The pattering feet with music sweet
And banners bright, and great delight
        That thou didst look upon.

One[1] honoured thee when o'er her thou didst wave
Thine ancient branches. There she oft did sit
Whose presence was as sunshine gladdening all
She looked upon. She was God's messenger,
Carolling glad truths like blythsome bird,

Or speaking words in season, softly, lovingly,
And telling forth the honour of her King.—
    My sister's work is done! She has passed away.
And thou *hast* fallen! both leaving us the record sure
Of thy Creator LORD, that He remains.

ELLEN P. SHAW.

WINTERDYNE.

[1] F. R. H.

(The grand cedar tree, where Kitty climbed, suddenly fell, uprooted in the gale of wind, October 14th, 1881.) [See page 74 of this book. That was the frontispiece of the original Nisbet edition of this book.]

FRANCIE'S OWN TUNE.

From Grandpapa Havergal, Sept. 14, 1860.

Pus - sy cat, pus - sy cat,   come   to   my   house;

You   shall   have   milk   e - nough,   you   shall   have   mouse:

I   will   not   tease   you   nor   hurt   you   in   play,

Nor   let   the   naugh - ty   dogs   drive   you   a - way.

Pussy cat, pussy cat, come to my lap;
Purr away, purr away, take a nice nap;
When you awake I will stroke you so pretty;
And I will call you my sweet little Kitty.

A KITTEN STORY.

SUCH a life as that kitten led me! I thought I never should have got her home at all, and yet I could not leave her to be starved or teased by urchins and dogs.

But I must tell you all about it from the beginning.

Passing through the village[1] this morning, I heard a kitten mewing most dismally. I looked all around, but could not see her anywhere, so I went on. In a little while I came back the same way, and still these miserable mews were to be heard. So I spied about more carefully, and at last I saw a poor little kitten on the top of a very high garden wall. It was a very pretty little tabby, with a white nose and four little white paws and a little white waistcoat. I can't imagine how it ever got up there; anyhow it could not get down again, and this was why it was mewing so dolefully. Neither do I know why the kitten expected *me* to come and get her down, but she evidently did. There was no doubt about that, if you had seen how she looked at me and stretched her little white paws down to me over the edge of the wall. She was quite out of my reach, but I stood close under and held up my hands, and called "Kitty, Kitty," thinking she would jump down into them.

But instead of doing that, she seemed to think it was too far to jump, though she nearly fell over by stretching her little paws down and holding on by her claws. And then she mewed more pitifully than ever, just as if she were saying, "Oh dear, oh dear, I daren't jump! I'm afraid you wouldn't catch me, and I should tumble down. Oh dear, oh dear, I wish I dared jump! whatever *shall* I do?" "Come, Kitty, come then!" said I. "Mew, mew!" said she. "Come now, jump, Kitty, and I'll be sure to catch you," said I. "Mew, mew, mew!" said she.

Well, I really couldn't stay there all day, so I said, "Well then, if you *won't* trust me to catch you, I must go away," and off I walked. Whereupon Kitty sent such a mew after me that you could have heard her all down the street. I could not stand that, so I turned back once more. Whom should I see coming up but a tall strong boy. "Why, Davie, you are the very person I want! Climb up by the gate, that's a good fellow, and get that unfortunate kitten down." So Davie climbed up, and the kitten had the sense to walk off the wall on to his shoulder without any more ado, and in a minute was safe on the ground.

---

[1] The Mumbles. [The Mumbles was a small village where F.R.H. lived, near Swansea, on the southern coast of Wales.]

"I put her inside the garden gate and set off home. But before I had gone three steps I nearly tumbled over her! She had run after me, and was purring under my feet. I told her to go back, but she only purred louder, and rubbed round my feet. No, she did not mean to be sent back. She was too much obliged to me for listening to her cry. I could not possibly scold her, so I picked her up and took her to the house which I supposed was her home. But no, it was not their kitten; perhaps it belonged next door. So I tried next door, but she was not owned there, nor at the next house. It was getting late, and I could not go back to any more houses. So I put her down, hoping she would find her own way and let me go mine. But she trotted after me, and it was not the least use talking to her. So I went faster; then she went faster too. Then I went quick round a corner, out of her sight. How that little cat did use her voice, to be sure! Such a mew she set up! And she did not only mew, she scampered, so that I saw it was no good trying to outrun her.

By this time we had come so far that I thought there was nothing for it but to let her follow me home and give her some milk, for she looked thin and hungry. Just then a little boy came by, who looked at her a moment and quickly stooped down and caught her up. "Does she belong to you?" I asked. "No, miss," he said, and seemed rather ashamed of himself. "Then you put her down directly," I said. And Kitty, who did not seem at all happy at being laid hold of so roughly, trotted on by my side.

But the path was very rough with sharp fresh stones, and Kitty's little feet looked much too soft for such work, so I took her up and carried her. At first she was quite delighted, and purred away, rubbing her little white nose into my sleeve. And we got on a great deal faster too, because she was not always hindering me by getting just under my feet, or lagging behind and then mewing for me to stop for her. And I am sure no kitten could have wished to be more comfortable, nursed in my arms on a soft sealskin muff! But very soon she got restless and wanted to jump down. "Now you had better be still, Kitty," I said, "you don't know when you are well off." But she would jump down, and I am sure it must have hurt her little soft paws to jump right down on those sharp stones, though she did not own to it! However she did hinder so that I told her she must be carried if we were to get home at all, and took her up again. No, she liked her own way best and would not lie still, though I know she found the stones very uncomfortable, and had to keep mewing not to be left behind. But I thought it was time I had *my* way with her, so I covered her with my hand so that she could not wriggle away.

But how she did wriggle! It was no use telling her what nice milk she should have when I had carried her home, she did not understand anything about that. "But I knew she was very hungry; and determined not to let her go and most likely be starved to death in the cold lanes if I did. Still she wriggled so that once more I let her jump down. But this time a disagreeable looking dog appeared, and, whether she liked it or not, I was not going to let her run the risk of being snapped at and perhaps bitten, so once more I picked her up. But in her fright at the dog she ran through some mud, and if I had not been very anxious to save her I would not have had her dirty little paws in my arms. But as I was very anxious to save her I wiped the mud off and wrapped her little feet in my handkerchief, and told her, once for all, I was *not* going to let her out of my arms any more till we were safe home.

Now you would have thought I should have no more trouble with her, stupid little thing! But the next thing was that we passed some sheep. What sort of dreadful monsters she took them to be I can't tell you, but she was more frightened at them than at the dog. She was so frightened that it was all I could do to hold her; she pushed and wriggled, and I could feel her little heart beating with terror. That was the most foolish thing of all, for if they had been such dangerous beasts as she seemed to suppose she would have been perfectly safe in my arms, and certainly she would not have been safe down on the ground, for what can a poor little kitten do to defend itself against animals twenty times bigger?

At last she gave in, and lay still all the rest of the way, and then I know she found it much nicer than being so fidgety, for she did nothing but purr till we reached the door. And she purred all the time she lapped up her milk, and except going to sleep I don't think she has done anything else but purr all day. And she is purring in my lap now, while I am writing this. . . .

[This kitten story was written in the spring of 1879, the cat story in 1869, both showing F. R. H.'s love for animals. The kitten story can *never* be finished, for the dear hand will never write any more. Let us think that if our dear F. R. H. was so glad to rescue and comfort little Kitty we too should be kind to all God's creatures. And why should not children always be purring and praising? Then how happy nurseries would be! Then, as little Kitty loved the dear hand that brought her home and petted her, cannot you try to be more loving to dear mother's gentle hand, and even think how much trouble nursey's hands have with you.

Above all let us love the wonderful hand of Jesus, that so tenderly reaches us when lost and in soul danger; the hand that will hold yours all the way to His bright home; the hand that was pierced and bleeding to save you.

> Oh how good is Jesus!
> May He hold my hand,
> And at last receive me
> To the better land.
>
> M. V. G. H.]

BIBLE FLOWER MISSION.

The readers of "Something to Do" will like to know where they can send bouquets and texts for distribution.

*Flowers will be thankfully received at any Hospital or Workhouse, or at the following London Depots:—*Miss Bewsher, 3, Clyde Street, London; 110, *Cannon Street, E.C.; Home of Industry, 60, Commercial Street, Spitalfields, E.; Conference Hall, Mildmay Park, N.*

Hampers and parcels (carriage paid) should be addressed: "Secretary, Bible Flower Mission."

———

N.B.—It is a great help when the flowers are made up into small bouquets. They travel best when packed dry with the stalks downward. Hampers should be lined with paper to exclude the air.

Something to Do.

"SOMETHING to do, mamma, something to do!"
　　Who has not heard the cry?
　　Something to plan and something to try!
Something to do when the sky is blue,
　　And the sun is clear and high;
Something to do on a rainy day,
Tired of lessons or tired of play;
Something to do in the morning walk,
Better than merely to stroll and talk.
For the fidgetty feet, oh, something to do,
For the mischievous fingers something too;
For the busy thought in the little brain,
　　For the longing love of the little heart,
Something easy, and nice, and plain;
　　Something in which they can all take part;
Something better than breakable toys;
Something for girls and something for boys!
I know, I know, and I'll tell you too,
Something for all of you now to do!

First, you must listen! Do you know
Where the poor sick children go?
Think of hundreds all together
In the pleasant summer weather,
Lying sadly day by day,
Having pain instead of play;
No dear mother sitting near,
　　No papa to kiss good night;
Brothers, sisters, playmates dear,
　　All away and out of sight.
Little feet that cannot go
Where the pink-tipped daisies grow;
Little eyes that never see
Bud or blossom, bird or tree,

Little hands that folded lie
As the weary weeks go by.
What if you could send them flowers
Brightening up the dismal hours?

Then the hospitals for others,
For the fathers and the mothers;
Where the weary sufferers lie
    While the weeks go slowly past,
    Some with hope of cure at last,
Some to suffer till they die.
Now, while you are scampering free,
In your happy springtide glee,
They are lying sadly there,
Weak and sick,—Oh, don't you care?
Don't you want to cheer each one?
Don't you wish it could be done?

Then the poor old people too,
    In the dreary workhouse-room,
Nothing all day long to do,
    Nothing to light up the gloom!
Older, weaker every day,
All their children gone away;
Nothing pleasant, nothing bright,
For the dimming aching sight.
Would it not be nice to send
Nosegays by some loving friend?

Then if you could only see
    Where so many thousands live,
All in sin and misery,
Dirt and noise and poverty,
    What, oh what, would you not give,
Just some little thing to do
    That might do a little good!
Don't you want to help them too?
    I will tell you how you could!
Gather flowers for Jesus' sake,
For a loving hand to take

Into all those dreadful places,
Bringing smiles to haggard faces,
Bringing tears to hardened eyes;
Bringing back the memories
Of the home so long ago
Left for wickedness and woe,
Of the time so far away
When they learnt to sing and pray.
Oh, you cannot guess the power
Of a little simple flower!

And yet the message they should bear,
Of God our Father's love and care,
Is never really read aright
Without the Holy Spirit's light;—
Without the voice of Jesus, heard
In His own sweet and mighty word
And so we *never* send the flowers
With only messages of ours;
But every group of buds and bells
The story of salvation tells.
Let every little nosegay bring
Not only fragrance of the spring,
But sweeter fragrance of His Name,
    Who saves and pardons, soothes and heals,
The living Saviour, still the Same,
    Who every pain and sorrow feels.
The little texts are sweeter far
Than lily-bell or primrose star;
And He will help you just to choose
The very words that He will use.
Now will it not be real delight
    To find them out and make a list
Of promise-words, so strong and bright,
So full of comfort and of light,
    That all their meaning *can't* be missed?
Think how every one may be
    God's own message from above
To some little girl or boy,
Changing sadness into joy,

Soothing some one's dreadful pain,
Making some one glad again,
    With His comfort and His love!
Calling them to Jesus' feet,
    Showing them what He has done!
Darlings, will it not be sweet
    If He blesses only one!
Only *one?* Nay, ask Him still,
    Ask Him *every one* to bless!
He can do it, and He will;
    Do not let us ask Him less!

Now then, set to work at once,
If you're not a thorough dunce!
Cut the little holders squarely,
    Keep the edges smooth and straight:
Now the paint box: artists bold,
    Paint the borders firm and fairly
With your prettiest red or gold!
    Easy this, at any rate.
Now for writing—clearest, neatest.
    (Or it may be gently hinted,
    Better still, if neatly printed.)
Tracing words the strongest, sweetest,—
Words that must and will avail,
Though the loveliest blossoms fail.

Then away, away, the first fine day!
Follow the breeze that is out at play,
Follow the bird and follow the bee,
Follow the butterfly flitting free,
    For I think they know
Where the sweetest wildflowers grow;
Bluebells in the shady dingle,
Where the violet odours mingle;
Where the fairy primrose lamp
    Seems to light the hawthorn shade;
Orchis in the meadow damp,
    Cowslip in the sunny glade.

(But not the pale anemone,
For that will fade so speedily.)
Hedge and coppice, lane and field;
Gather all the store they yield!
Buttercups and daisies too,
Though so little prized by you,
Will be gold and silver treasure
In their power of giving pleasure
To the poor in city alleys,
Far away from hills and valleys,
Who have never seen them grow
Since their childhood, long ago;
Or to children pale and small,
Who never saw them grow at all!
And don't forget the fair green leaves
    That have their own sweet tales to tell,
And waving grass that humbly weaves
    The emerald robe of bank and dell.

Is there some one at home who cannot go
To gather the flowers as they grow?
Then there is plenty for her to do
In making the nosegays up for you;
Getting them ready to travel away,
In time for the work of the coming day.

But oh how busy you will be
    When the packing must be done;
Oh the bustle and the glee,
    Will it not be famous fun!
And when the box is gone away
    The pleasure need not all be past;
    I think it will not be the last!
Just set to work another day,
    And send some more
    From the beautiful store
Which God keeps sending you fresh and new,
    And thank Him too
That He has given you "SOMETHING TO DO!"

CONNIE'S CHICKENS.

ONCE upon a time there was a little girl named Connie. Not very far from her home there was a very large old barn, with old black beams and an old thatched roof. In this barn lived an old hen. She was Connie's very own; and so, when seven little chickens were hatched, they were Connie's very own too. One evening, just as Connie was going to bed, she heard people running and shouting, and when she looked out of the window she saw a bright light flickering through the trees, and in a very few minutes, as the light got bigger and brighter, and great flames began to fork up into a great cloud of smoke, she knew that the old barn was on fire. Her little sister began to cry, and Connie was just going to begin too; when, all at once, she turned away from the sight of the blaze, and went and knelt down in a corner of the nursery, and said: "O God, please don't let my little chickens be burnt! oh, *don't* let my little chickens be burnt; for Jesus Christ's sake, amen."

The gracious Friend above heard Connie's prayer for her "little chickens," and answered it too. Nobody ever knew exactly how they got out of the barn, and of course the old hen could not tell her story; but next morning, when the fire was out, because every bit of the poor old barn was burnt down, the old hen and her seven little chickens were found, all safe and sound, clucking and scratching in the orchard beyond, just as if nothing had happened.

Now, whenever you think of Connie's "little chickens," I want you to recollect a little text. The Lord Jesus said, "How much more are ye better than the fowls?" And if He heard a little girl's prayer, and saved the poor little fowls from the blazing barn, will He not much more save you?

ROBIN REDBREAST AND THE BROWN MOUSE.

Such a cold morning! Such a white world outside! Snow on the grass, and snow on the path, and snow on the ivy round the window, and more snow coming in great quiet flakes, and the sky all full of snow-clouds!

It was warm and cosy in the parlour where Ellie had her breakfast; no snow and no cold wind could come in there. But what about the robin that had been singing all the autumn in the shrubbery? He had had a very pleasant summer of it, with plenty to eat, and plenty to sing about. But now that the snow was come, what would he do? His pretty red feathers and his clever songs would not keep the little gentleman from starving, any more than if he were a common little sparrow that only knew how to chirp and had no handsome dress at all.

So Ellie opened the window, and put some crumbs all along the sill, and drew back a little so that Master Robin might not be afraid to come for them. Presently he spied them. He was very hungry, poor fellow, in spite of his scarlet waistcoat. So he put his head on one side and looked at them, and then he hopped on to another bough a little nearer, and looked at them again. He did not quite like going close up, he did not quite trust that open window, it might suddenly shut down and catch him, and he was not sure about Ellie's intentions. Wasn't he silly? He hopped a little farther off. The snow might be gone in a day or two, and he might manage to get on better. Yes, but it might not be gone, and *the crumbs might be gone*—it might be now or never. And he was very hungry.

So at last he hopped down to the lowest branch, and then on to the ground, and then, hop, hop, hop, on the window-sill—just the most sensible thing he could do. Once there, he found he was all right; the window was not a trap at all, and Ellie meant nothing but kindness. And the crumbs were so good that he made up his mind never to stop starving up in the boughs any more. How Master Robin did enjoy them, and how delighted Ellie was to feed him! For she knew much better than he did what a terrible death he must have died if he had been so foolish as to let himself be starved in the snow.

All at once there was a little rustle among the ivy leaves—such a very little rustle that even Master Robin was not frightened. And out crept a poor little brown mouse, with little sparkling black eyes—very, very frightened, so that even its little tail trembled; but so very, very hungry, that when it knew there were crumbs to be had it really couldn't help coming. And so it came; and there were plenty of crumbs for it as well as for the little singer, although it could not even chirp like the sparrow, but only knew how to squeak.

If Ellie was pleased to see the robin come and be fed, she was ten times more pleased to see this unexpected little guest. And to see them feeding both together, don't you think that was nice? What do you think she did? She thought as Mousie had been brave enough to trust her, he should have a good deal more than he ever expected. So she went and got a little bit of mince-pie, and when Mousie looked up from his crumbs and was just going to scamper away, what did he see but Ellie's hand putting some beautiful mincemeat almost close to his little cold nose! Mousie had too much sense to run off to his hole then, but stayed and had the best feast he ever had in his life, although the snow kept coming down. And if he and Robin could only have understood, they would have heard Ellie telling them that they need not ever be hungry again, for she would give them plenty of crumbs every day, no matter how long the snow lasted. All the same, they *did* understand somehow! and showed they understood by coming again.

Robin and Mousie had very different homes. Robin had a beautiful nest in a blossoming hawthorn tree, and had lived among the flowers and leaves and out in the sunshine. Mousie had lived in a little dark hole under an old wall. But the cold winter came to both their homes. And both had the same reason for going to Ellie's window,—they were very hungry. And both of them would have died if they had nothing to eat.

Is there not a little lesson in this about coming to the Lord Jesus? "The rich and the poor meet together" in coming to Him. The girl or boy who lives in a handsome house, and has nice clothes, and is taught all sorts of clever things; and the girl or boy who lives in the poorest little dark room, and wears a very old frock or jacket, and is not clever at all, must both come to Jesus, one just as much as the other, and for just the same reason, and in just the same way. The reason is, because you will perish if you do not come. Yes, really perish! really go away into the outer darkness, where will be weeping and gnashing of teeth! It seems so terrible to have to tell you this, but it is *true*. Some people think it quite unkind to mention it. But the really unkind thing would be *not* to tell you; to let you go on not knowing or not thinking about it. Perhaps the Lord Jesus has sent you this little book on purpose to make you think about it, and to make you want to be saved. *Don't* you want to be saved? Don't you want to have all the cold, terrible, dark uncertainty taken away, and to know that you, your very own self, are "Safe in the arms of Jesus"? Don't you sometimes feel like being *hungry* to know it? Well now, why need you feel hungry about it any

longer? Was it not very foolish of Robin to stay hopping about the cold branches, feeling hungry, and seeing the crumbs all put ready for him, and yet not going at once? And was it not very wise of little Mousie to creep out straight to
them as soon as ever he saw them? Now, if you are hungry, do not wait hopping about, but just come at once to Jesus. Tell Him all about it. Tell Him you
want to be saved. Tell Him you hardly know what you want, but you know you
want something and you want *Him*.

One Sunday a friend of mine saw a poor little boy, only six years old, crying
bitterly. He said: "Well, my little man, what are you crying for? what do you
want?" I know how glad my friend was at the little boy's answer, for he sobbed
out, "Please, sir, I want Jesus!" Nobody ever wanted Jesus but what Jesus wanted them. And so, before the next Sunday came, the little fellow's tears were all
gone; and next time the kind clergyman met him he could hardly say the words
quick enough for joy, "Please, sir, I've found Jesus!"

So, if you want Jesus, remember He wants you; just as Ellie wanted the little bird to come and be fed.

There was a poor man in Ireland who listened for the first time to the story you know so well, of how the Lord Jesus came to save us, and of His exceeding great love. And instead of waiting to hear it over and over again, as some of
you do, he believed it at once, and said "Glory be to God!" And then, with his
ragged hat off, he went to the preacher and said, "Thank you, sir; you've taken
the hunger off us to-day." You see it came true, what Jesus said so long ago, "He
that cometh to Me shall never hunger." And it will come true for you directly
you come to Him; He will "take the hunger off you."

You may thank God at once if He has made you "want Jesus" at all. For it
is only the Holy Spirit that ever makes any one hungry for Him. I never heard
a sadder answer than a young lady gave me the other day. She said, "No, I don't
want Jesus; at least, not yet." She wanted all sorts of other things, but not Jesus.
Are any of you saying that in your hearts? Oh, what will you do without Him?
What will you do when the day, not of wintry snow, but of fiery terror, is come?
You will want Him then, when "the great day of His wrath is come," but it will
be too late. Will you not pray, "Lord Jesus, make me want Thee now"?

> Why should you do without Him?
> It is not yet too late;
> He has not closed the day of grace,
> He has not shut the gate.
> He calls you! Hush! He calls you!
> He would not have you go

Another step without Him,
    Because He loves you so.

Why will you do without Him?
    He calls and calls again—
"Come unto Me! Come unto Me!"
    Oh, shall He call in vain?
He wants to have you with Him;
    Do you not want Him too?
You cannot do without Him,
    And He wants—even you.

"WHO WILL TAKE CARE OF ME?"

From

F. R. H.

to

Emily F. W. W. Snepp:

Jan. 1, 1873.

Music and Words by Frances Ridley Havergal, specially composed for Miss Snepp.[1]

---

[1] This tune is given, as "EUNICE," in the New Musical Edition of "SONGS OF GRACE AND GLORY," page 428.
[See page 984 of Volume V of the Havergal edition.]

"Who Will Take Care of Me?"

"He hath said, I will never leave thee, nor forsake thee."—Hebrews 13:5.

"Who will take care of me?" darling, you say!
  Lovingly, tenderly, watched as you are!
Listen! I give you the answer today,
  One who is never forgetful or far!

He will take care of you! All through the day
  Jesus is near you, to keep you from ill;
Walking or resting, at lessons or play,
  Jesus is with you and watching you still.

He will take care of you! All through the night
  Jesus, the Shepherd, His little one keeps;
Darkness to Him is the same as the light,
  He never slumbers, and *He* never sleeps.

He will take care of you! All through the year,
  Crowning each day with His kindness and love,
Sending you blessings and shielding from fear,
  Leading you on to the bright home above.

He will take care of you! Yes, to the end,
  Nothing can alter His love to His own.
Darling, be glad that you have such a Friend,
  He will not leave you one moment alone.

TO DEARIE.

I AM so pleased with your report. I am sure you must have tried hard, to earn such a good one the *first* term, for of course everything is hardest at first. One item thoroughly *surprises me*; the "very satisfactory indeed" for French conversation, and it is very satisfactory *indeed* to me, because I am sure French conversation does not "come natural" to you, and that this must imply a great deal of *steadily trying* to do what is not very easy, and most likely not very pleasant as yet to you, though every week at school will make it easier.

The report under "Bible" you may be quite sure makes me very glad indeed, and the "almost perfect" repetition is fulfilling one of my great wishes for you, "that the word of Christ may dwell in you richly," and filling your memory with it is a great step towards filling your heart and then your very life with it. The Scripture I know by heart is my most valuable mental treasure.[1]

Well, now about the one exception to the otherwise good report! Do you see, dearie, that the great thing you (and I too) want to learn is to *yield*, to give up our own wills, our own dislike to *have* to do what we don't exactly like; this is a great deal more than any other learning, and only God can teach it us. Now if we only had to do with and give up to people whom we like very much, we should never really learn to give in at all! And perhaps that is why God has permitted it so, that you should have one teacher whom you do not like to obey

---

[1] From F. R. H.'s Bible *some* of the chapters she learnt by heart are now given; besides the whole of the Psalms, the four Gospels, and many typical and historical chapters and the minor prophets. In 1846 she learned Isaiah 12, 53, 55. In 1854 the Epistle to the Romans. In 1856 first chapter of Genesis, learned in Hebrew; also Isaiah 1. In 1857 F. R. H. learned:

Epistle to the Hebrews	finished Oct. 24.
Epistle of James	Nov. 9.
1st Epistle of Peter	Nov. 25.
2nd Epistle of Peter	Dec. 5.
1st Epistle of John	Dec. 22.
2nd Epistle of John	Dec. 24.
3rd Epistle of John	Dec. 26.
Romans, relearned	Dec.
Jude	Dec. 30.
Galatians	Feb. 6, 1858.

Hence ten epistles learnt in five months!

for her own sake, so that He may give you the opportunity of acting as a really Christian girl, and quietly obeying and submitting for His own sake. Dearie, we want to obey our dear Master in every little thing; now will you just take His own word about it. Just hear what He says: "Submit yourselves to every ordinance of man *for the Lord's sake*, whether it be to the king as supreme, or unto governors," which includes governesses! It makes all the difference to think of those words *"for the Lord's sake"*; only think, that when Fraulein makes you do something you don't like, you have an opportunity given you which you would not otherwise have of submitting for Jesu's sake. We should not have thought of anything so grand and sweet in connection with such a little thing as "submitting" to hold your hands, or use your fingers, in a way you don't like, but there it is written in His word for you! If we only have teachers whom one naturally loves, one has no opportunity either of asking and being enabled to love them, and be patient for Jesu's sake. I have known more than one touching case, where a foreign governess was thought cross and "horrid," and the girls were cross and horrid to her in return, when the real reason was that she was so sad and depressed at being so far from home, and so utterly lonely, and had so many other trials of which she could not tell any one, that she could not rouse herself to be very bright at first, and that made the girls take a dislike which added bitterly to her trials, and kept her head under water. Only think how you would feel, if you had to go next term to Germany, with no friend near, and not an idea of going home at all for twelve months! Would you not be thankful if your pupils felt a little bit sorry for you, and tried to be kind to you?

I know you will find it a wonderful help, if you will ask Him to conquer for you where you have failed, to take away altogether all the *unloving* feeling to Fraulein, if there is any, and enable you really to please Him, by doing exactly what He tells you to do, "submit." I know He can do this so completely that you will be astonished, if you ask Him and trust Him to do it for you.

F. R. H.

TO EMMELINE.

OAKHAMPTON, *June 7th.*

MY DEAR LITTLE FELLOW-WORKER:

I have had a good many pleasant surprises in the course of my Irish collect-ing, but I don't recollect that I *ever* had a greater or pleasanter one than yours. You have actually beaten Bruey herself, for she had forty-one and you have forty-four names; and I have never but *once* had more than that from any one! I wonder if this is your first attempt at working for Christ. I think, dear Em-meline, Jesus Himself knows all about it, knows that you have been trying to be a little worker for Him. Isn't that very nice? And now I will ask Him to send a *great* blessing on what you have collected, so that those who are taught, by means of your money, may not only learn to read of Jesus in His word, but may learn to love Him and tell others about Him.

Perhaps you have done even more for the Irish Society than you think for, because you have put an idea in my head: Three little girls lately wrote me a let-ter, something like your first one, having liked "Bruey" so much. I was not well enough to answer at the time, but now I shall write and send them each a book, and make the same request I did to you, and then *possibly* they *too* may go to work and send more than the value of the books. I will send you a postcard to tell you if they do, because, you see, it will be really your doing if they also col-lect. I am writing to the Irish Society at Dublin to-day, and will ask them to send you one of the new Reports which will soon be ready, but unfortunately your name will not be in till next year. You will find my collectors and subscrib-ers near the end, under Leamington, and you will see there Miss K. Blanshard, the *only* one who has ever had more names than you, so I will tell about her.

She is a young invalid, and has been lying on her back for nearly three years. Just a year ago I was going to see her one day, and prayed that the Lord Jesus would help me to say something that would comfort and brighten her. And then He seemed to put it into my mind that if I could only think of some work for Christ for her to do, it would do her more good than anything. So I put a green card in my pocket. On the way I met a friend who said, "If you are not very busy, do go and see poor Katie, she does so want you to come." So I told her I was going. When I got there, Katie told me she had been asking our dear

Master all day to send me to her. So I asked her why she wanted me so particularly. Then she told me she had been feeling so sad to think she could do nothing for Jesus, and she had been praying for a whole week that He would let her do just some little thing for Him. So I took out the green card and told her I thought He had guided me to bring her a bit of work to do, and would she try and collect just a little for these poor Irish who can't be reached by people who can only speak English! So she was delighted, and took it as His own answer, and has ever considered it as the work He had given her to do for Him.

May I send my special thanks to your dear mamma both for allowing you to collect, and for so kindly helping you.

Your loving friend,

FRANCES R. HAVERGAL.

I am so much better.

P.S.—*Friday.* Thanks to your mamma for her postcard. Will you give her the enclosed little book? I must tell you how it happens that I have nothing to enclose to you. My dear little twin nephews, Willie and Ethelbert Havergal are staying here; both have quite decided to be clergymen when they grow up, and I think they are trying to be "little workers for Christ" already. A day or two ago they spied a drawer where I keep my ammunition, "little books and tracts and texts." "Oh, Aunt Fanny," said E., "will you let us have two or three? we *do* so like giving tracts away." So I said they "might take anything they liked," and they rummaged with great delight. Presently W. found some ornamental text cards, and said to E., "We won't take those, they are too good. Aunt Fanny could not have really meant it." So after a few more assurances they ended by completely clearing out *everything* they liked, *just taking me at my word.* They began by giving some Scripture leaflets to all the servants, and are looking forward to how nice it will be to give all these away to the people in papa's parish. I thought their taking me at my word was quite a little parable; but I cannot stay to tell you how, perhaps you can find out, and if not, perhaps your mamma will tell you.—F. R. H.

Little Norah.[1]

FAR off upon a western shore,
  Where wildest billows roam,
Beneath the great grim rocks there stands
  A tiny cabin home;

And in it dwells a little one,
  With eyes of laughing blue,
And lips as red as any rose
  With early sparkling dew.

Her father was a fisher, and
  Went out with every tide,
While Norah sat and watched alone
  By her sick mother's side.

It was a weary thing to sit
  For many a long, long day,
Without a ramble on the beach,
  Or e'en a thought of play;

But Norah did not think it hard,
  She loved her mother so,
And in a thousand ways she tried
  Her earnest love to show.

One day she left the cabin door,
  And walked a long, long way—
Now high upon the breezy cliffs,
  Now close to ocean spray.

She went to seek some remedy
  To ease her mother's pain,

---

[1]Also published by J. and R. Parlane, Paisley. Profits for the "Havergal Hall," Limerick, and the Bruey Branch.

Though little hope there was that she
    Could e'er be well again.

The ruby clouds have curtained o'er
    The golden glowing west,
Where 'neath the white-winged wavelets now
    The sun hath gone to rest;

But little Norah comes not yet!
    The mother's fears arise,
The evening breeze brings nothing save
    The seabird's mournful cries.

The twilight hour is passing fast,
    In weariness and pain;
She waits and listens for her child,
    As yet she waits in vain.

Hark, hark! a bounding step is heard
    Along the pebbly shore,
And now a tiny hand is laid
    Upon the cabin door.

"Oh, mother, darling mother, I
    Have such good news to tell;
Far more than medicine I have brought
    To make you glad and well."

More brightly gleamed her joyous eye,
    And rosier grew her cheek,
While forth she poured the happy words
    As fast as tongue could speak.

"I bought the medicine, mother dear,
    And turned to come away,
When by me stood a kind grave man,
    And gently bade me stay;

"And then he spoke sweet words to me,
    About the Saviour's love,
And of the glorious home where all
    His children meet above.

" He told me Jesus loved us so
    That He came down to die,
And suffered all instead of us;—
    And then it made me cry;

" He said His blood was quite enough
    To wash our sins away,
And make us fit for heaven at once
    If we should die to-day.

" So, mother dear, we shall not need
    To purgatory go;
If Jesus has forgiven all,
    That is enough, you know!"

The rosy glow had rested on
    The mother's whitening cheek;
'Twas fading now, and Norah ceased—
    Then came a long wild shriek,—

" Oh, mother, speak to me once more,—
    Oh, is she really dead?"
'Twas even so, the hand was cold,
    And stilled the throbbing head;

Yes, even while those blessed words
    Like angel music fell,
Her weary spirit passed away;
    But whither! Who may tell?

Oh, bitter were the tears that fell
    From little Norah's eye,
And many a day and night had passed
    Ere they again were dry.

But bitterest were they when she thought
    " Oh I can never tell
If with that blessed Saviour now,
    Sweet mother, thou dost dwell!

" Ah! had I only sooner known
    What I have heard to-day,

I would have told her more of Him
    Before she went away;

"For perhaps she did not hear me then,
    So she could never know
The way that Jesus Christ has made
    To His bright home to go.

"I love Him, yes, I'm sure I do;
    Then He will take me home
To be with Him for evermore,
    Where sorrow cannot come;

"But oh, I cannot bear to think,
    When I His glory see,
And rest within the Saviour's arms—
    Where will my mother be?"

Dear children, you have learnt the way
    To that bright home above,
You have been told of Jesus and
    His deep and tender love;

In Ireland there are little ones
    Whose hearts are very sad;
Oh, won't you try and send to them
    Sweet words to make them glad?

Dec. 1856.

"The going in of Thy words giveth light, giving understanding to the guideless."—Psalm 119:130 (*Irish rendering.*)

"Come over and Help Us."

The Irish child's cry.

Oh, children of England beyond the blue sea,
Your poor little brothers and sisters are we;
'Tis not much affection or pity we find,
But we hear you are loving and gentle and kind;
So will you not listen a minute or two,
While we tell you a tale that is all of it true?

We live in a cabin, dark, smoky and poor;
At night we lie down on the hard dirty floor;
Our clothes are oft tattered, and shoes we have none;
Our food we must beg, as we always have done;
So cold, and so hungry, and wretched are we,
It would make you quite sad if you only could see.

There's no one to teach us poor children to read;
There's no one to help us, and no one to lead;
There's no one at all that will tell us the way
To be happy or safe, or teach us to pray;
To the bright place above us we all want to go,
But we cannot, for how to get there we don't know.

They tell us the Virgin will hear if we call,
But sure in one minute she can't hear us all.
And the saints are too busy in heaven we hear;
Then often the priests make us tremble with fear
At the fire of purgatory, which, as they tell,
Is almost as dreadful as going to hell.

Oh, will you not help us, and send us a ray
Of the light of the gospel, to brighten our way?
Oh, will you not tell us the beautiful story
Of Jesus, who came from His dwelling of glory

To save little children, and not only you,
But even the poor ragged Irish ones too?

The English child's reply.

WE have heard the call from your fair green Isle,
  Our hearts have wept at your saddening tale,
And we long to waken a brighter smile,
  By a story of love which shall never fail.

We should like you to come to our Bible land,
  And share our comforts and blessings too;
We would take you all with a sister's hand,
  And try to teach and to gladden you.

But you're so far off that it cannot be,
  And we have no wings, or to you we'd fly,
So we'll try to send o'er the foaming sea
  Sweet words to brighten each heavy eye,

Sweet words of Him who was once so poor
  That He had not where to lay His head;
But hath opened now the gleaming door
  To the palace of light, where His feast is spread.

There you may enter; He calls each one,
  You're as welcome there as the greatest king;
Come to Him then, for He casts out none,
  And nothing at all do you need to bring.

He will change your rags for a robe of white,
  An angel harp, and a crown of gold;
You may dwell for aye in His presence bright,
  And the beaming smiles of His love behold.

We will gladly save from our little store
  Our pennies, our farthings, from day to day,
And only wish we could do far more;
  But for Erin's children we'll always pray.

1856.

"HOW MUCH FOR JESUS?"

A LITTLE group of boys and girls were gathered around me on a pleasant evening in the Easter holidays. We were talking about the Lord Jesus, and all the wonderful and solemn things which our Church services had so lately brought before us; His agony and bloody sweat, His cross and passions, His precious death and burial, and His glorious resurrection. There was such a quieted and tender tone among them, such wistful looks and gentle voices; and the hearts of more than one were so evidently burning within them, that one could not doubt that "Jesus Himself drew near," and that while we spoke one to another He not only hearkened and heard, but was really present in our midst.

Then we spoke of what we owed to Him who had done so much for us. How much do we owe Him? and how much shall we give Him?

Can there be any hesitation as to the answer? Shall it not be, joyfully and gratefully, "All! yes, *all* for Jesus!"

But "all" means a great deal; it really does mean *all*; all our hearts, all our lives, all that we have, all that we are. And if truly "all," it must be for *always* too; no reserve, and no taking back.

I heard a little sigh by my side as we spoke of this. Did it seem too hard? Could we ever hope to keep to it? Was it more than we dared say? Then we looked at the bright side of it, the grand shining of gladness which Satan tries to hinder us from seeing. If we are "all for Jesus," He will be all for us, and *always* all for us, too. When we give Him all, He gives us all; all His tender love, all His wonderful peace and joy, all His grace and strength. On His side there will be no reserve and no taking back. And with "all" this we shall find, nay we *do* find, that life is quite a different thing; ever so much happier than we imagined it could be, and that He does for us exceeding abundantly above all that we ask or think.

As this was dwelt upon, I saw a very bright smile on a face that was generally the merriest of the party. After a little while, "good-night" was said, and we separated. But I went upstairs to two quiet rooms. In the first I found the author of that little sigh. She was, I had every reason to hope, a dear Christian child, who had for some time past "known and believed the love which God hath for us," and had tried to follow her Saviour in the little steps of home and school life.

I put my arms round her, and said, "Well, A——, how much for Jesus?" The great dark eyes that just before had looked up so lovingly into my face fell, with such a mournful look that I shall never forget it. That was no answer. "How much, darling? Is it not *all* for Jesus? Again came the little sigh, and a sad whisper, "I don't know."

In the other room another warm kiss awaited me, and there was something in the merry face which made me ask quite hopefully, "Well, M—— how much for Jesus?"

Oh if I could describe to you the utter gladness in the bright eyes, and the very joy that seemed to overflow the lips, as she answered, not hastily but very firmly and resolutely, "All, auntie, all!" That too was a look never to be forgotten; the words and the tone were sweet and strong, but the look told more than either. One could not but take knowledge of her that she had been with Jesus. She had given her heart to Him, and He had given His joy to her.

Let me put the question to you—"How much for Jesus?" Is your answer a sigh or a smile?

ONLY one heart to give,
    Only one voice to use;
Only one little life to live,
    And only one to lose.

All! for far more I owe
    Than all I have to bring;
All! for my Saviour loves me so;
    All! for I love my King.

Poor is my best, and small:
    How could I dare divide?
Surely my Lord shall have it all,
    He shall not be denied.

All! for it is His own,
    He gave the tiny store;
All! for it must be His alone;
    All! for I have no more.

All! for the last and least
    He stoopeth to uplift:
The altar of my great High Priest
    Shall sanctify my gift.

[*Hymn Chant* THYATIRA.]

LITTLE LIFEBOAT HELPERS.

"The lifeboat is going out to practise at ten o'clock."

So away we hurried to the harbour. The Union Jack was flying on the top of the large shed where the lifeboat was kept, and a crowd had collected opposite the great doors when we reached the quay.

Presently the doors were opened, and we got a peep of the bright boat, as white as the foam it was to ride over, with gay blue and scarlet sides and keel; and forthwith a great excitement arose among several dozen little boys, who set up a very lively hurrah. Then the crew gradually appeared, twelve strong fellows in dark blue clothes and scarlet caps with a rather Turkish look about them, each with a cork jacket fastened round him, so that sinking in any sea was out of the question.

In a few minutes the lifeboat, mounted on high wheels, was pulled and pushed slowly out of the shed on to the quay, and the small boys cheered more energetically still. There she was, ready to save in any sea, with festoons of rope all round her sides, so that any poor drowning man could catch and hold on if once within reach; and the brave, bronze-faced crew, ready to go out in the wildest storm and stretch out their strong hands to those who must perish without such help.

But there she was, with her blue and white oars lying useless, for she was a hundred yards from the water. And how was she to be dragged to the edge, where she could be launched out and row away to her work?

Those little fellows knew all about it, and were eagerly looking out for their share in the work! All at once one of the scarlet capped men threw a long thick rope from the boat into the road, and in a minute at least thirty little urchins had seized it, run it out to its full length with another cheer, and waited the signal to pull. Some of the rest looked disappointed because there was not room for them to get hold of it, but none of them went away; and in another minute a second rope was flung from the other side of the boat, hardly touching the ground before it was pounced upon by those who had missed the chance of the first rope. Then the red caps gave a great push all together, while the little lads watched the moment and pulled at the two ropes with all their might, and the great lifeboat, which would carry thirty shipwrecked men besides its own crew, began to move quite easily and quickly towards the beach.

It was splendid to see those sixty little fellows, hearty little Britons, enjoying the work which nobody set them or asked them to do, cheering and tugging away, not a single grown man among them, and yet doing what one would have expected to see grown men or even horses doing. There was one scrap of a boy in knickerbockers, not above five years old, slanting his body and straining his wee arms at the rope, as if the launch of the lifeboat depended on him. There were two or three shoeless mites, planting their bare toes against the stones, and pulling as hard as the most comfortably shod schoolboy among them.

In a very little while they had dragged the good boat to the beach; and then they scampered along the pier and had the delight of seeing her rowed fast and steadily by the redcaps out among the wild white waves, where, not so very far from the mouth of the harbour, many and many a collier vessel and fishing smack had been wrecked within sight of safety, but out of reach of any help till the lifeboat was provided.

Very likely some of those little lads will grow up and go out in the lifeboat themselves; but they don't wait for that, *they come and help all they can now.* Don't you think that when she comes back to the harbour with sailors and little cabin boys saved from drowning in that fierce roaring sea, these Whitby boys must be ten times more delighted than if they had had no hand in it, but had stood idly looking on, and letting other people do all the pulling!

Now what lifeboats are there to which you can give a pull? Quite certain to be one, very likely several, within your reach. There are wrecks going on night and day in the great sea of life, terrible wrecks of souls on every heathen shore, numbers drowning in sin close at hand. And brave men and women leave their warm homes and go out to them with the lifeboat of salvation, go right away into the waves, and stretch out their hands to draw them into the lifeboat. You are not old enough to go yet, but *you can help to start the lifeboats.*

Every time a missionary meeting or a Bible meeting is held, and the speaker tries to persuade you to do what you can, to have a collecting box, to give what you would spend on your own pleasure, and get others to do the same, it is like throwing out a rope for the little ones to pull at. And when many pull together it is surprising what a difference it makes. I have heard that twenty thousand pounds a year comes to the Church Missionary Society in sixpences alone. There must have been a good many little ones pulling at *that* rope!

What are you going to do? Stand by with your hands in your pockets and see the others pull, and say, "Yes, it is very interesting, and I hope the lifeboat will save a great many people"? No! look out for the ropes (they are always being thrown out), and shout to all your companions to come too, and then give "a long pull, and a strong pull, and a pull all together," and then even you will be little fellow workers in the great, glorious, happy work of saving souls from a more terrible death than they would meet in the cold waves of the North Sea at Whitby.

"I SAY UNTO YOU."

(Matthew 5:18)

SEE how many times these four little words come in to-day's and to-morrow's readings![1] What the Lord Jesus said so often, we surely ought to notice.

It makes all the difference *who* says a thing. If you could get near enough to the Queen to hear her say anything, you would listen with all your might. And if she began "I say," you would lean forward to make sure of hearing what she had to say. But if she said, "I say to *you*," I am sure no one would need to tell you to pay attention.

Now the Lord Jesus says, over and over again: "*I* say unto you." It was not only that He did say it a long time ago, but that whenever you look at the words He is saying it still. For His words are not dead; they are *live* words, just as much as if He had said them a minute ago. For He says "they are spirit and life," and that they shall "never pass away." So when you come to "I say unto you," remember Jesus means it, and that He really means you to pay the same attention to what comes next as if He were speaking aloud to you.

And then remember it always means "I say unto *you*"; not only the disciples who went up to Him in the mountain, but each of you who are just beginning to be one of His learners, for that is what "disciple" means. Some of the things He says may be a little more than you can understand yet, but they are said to you all the same. When I was a little girl I had a sovereign given me. If it had been a shilling I might have put it in my own little purse, and spent it at once; but, being a sovereign, my dear father took care of it for me, and I expect I forgot all about it. But one day when I was quite grown up, he called me into his study and gave me the sovereign, reminding me how it had been given me when I was about as high as the back of a chair. And I was very glad to have it then, for I understood how much it was worth, and knew very well what to do with it. Now, when you come to some saying of the Lord Jesus that you do not understand or see how to make any use of for yourself, do not think it of no consequence whether you read it or not. When you are older you will find that it is just like my sovereign, coming back to you, when you want it and are able to

[1] In the Children's Scripture Union, in connection with the Children's Special Service Mission.

make use of it. But how good it is of the Lord Jesus to have said so many things that are just what will help you now! Be on the look out for them every time you read, and see if you don't find something every day which is for you *now*. Ask for the Holy Spirit *always* before you begin, and then you may say as Habakkuk did, "I will watch to see what He will say unto me."

Suppose you keep a sharp-pointed pencil or a fine pen in the place where you usually read your Bible, and mark every time that the Lord Jesus says "I say unto you." And I think it would be a good plan if you put a double mark to every saying of His which you feel has come home to your own heart. You will remember them better, and it will help you to find them again.

WHITE ROBES.

Music by F. R. Havergal.

Oh, glorious land of light,
Where all is fair and bright,
Arrayed in robes of white
    Thy ransomed ones appear;
Across their radiant brow,
Grief flings no shadow now,
Beneath no cross they bow,
    Nor shed one transient tear.

White robes! not armour—no!
While militant below,
They fought with many a foe,
    And trod the tempter down;
But on life's battle field
They left their sword and shield,
And took—their wounds all healed—
    The conqueror's garb and crown!

White robes! their pilgrim dress,
Like that in which we press
Earth's path of weariness,
    Within their grave is cast;
And flowing raiment fair,
As child or bride might share
At home, sweet home, they wear;
    For all their toils are past.

White robes! our garments here
Too oft defiled appear;
But in the heaven that's near
    No sin its gladness taints;
And washed in streams that flow
To cleanse from guilt and woe,
Purer than winter snow
    Are the white robes of saints!

ARTHUR PHILLIPS.

"Therefore be ye also ready." (Matthew 24:44.)

I WONDER if you have heard of Miss Weston, and the good work she is doing among the sailors, and the interesting book she has written about them, called "Our Blue-jackets"? I will tell you about one of her Blue-jackets, Arthur Phillips, and how she came to know him.

She was staying with a friend at Plymouth, a place where there are a great many ships and sailors. And she saw that on Sunday afternoons there were numbers of sailor boys wandering about the streets, with no friends, and no place to go to, and nothing to do; so that it was no wonder if they got into bad company. She felt very sorry for them, and thought perhaps some of them had good mothers praying for them in some far-away home, and how troubled they must be when they thought of their boys with no one to care for them. So she set to work to see what she could do for them. She sent little notices to all the ships that the boys might come and meet her in a large room for singing and reading on Sunday afternoons. But an officer told her he was afraid it would be of no use; he said, "They are as restless when they come ashore as birds let out of a cage." And so, sure enough, after waiting two hours the first Sunday, only one lad came, and he was too frightened to stay all alone.

The next Sunday not one came, nor the next, nor the next. And then most persons would have said, "Oh, it's no use!" and given it up. But Miss Weston did not say that; she did the best thing anybody possibly can do when they are disappointed and puzzled, she "went and told Jesus" all about it. He knew how much she wanted to help these poor lads, and so He showed her another way to catch them.

The friend with whom she was staying offered the use of her kitchen for them, with tea and cake into the bargain. Then two good men offered to go out into the streets and try to bring them in. Very soon a dozen came, and they liked the tea and cake and cosy warm kitchen so much that they brought others, and then there were two dozen, and then three dozen, and they sat on the window ledge, and among the cups and saucers on the dresser, and even inside the grate, till before long the kitchen could not hold them at all.

It was not only for cake and tea that they came; they sang hymns and listened to their friend as she told them Bible stories and prayed with them. So the officer was wrong after all; perhaps he did not know how the story of the love of Jesus can make a restless sailor boy listen. Jesus said, "I, if I be lifted up, will draw all men unto Me," and you see how this came true, and even these wild lads, let loose from their ships, were drawn when He was lifted up among them.

Among those whom Jesus really drew to Himself was a fine young sailor named Arthur Phillips. Sunday after Sunday he was always at the meeting. As regularly as the clock struck three, he might be seen with his happy sunburnt face, coming up the garden path, bringing two or three others with him. When the kitchen got too full he would say, "Well, we are crowded out; we shall soon have to ask God to give us a larger place, Miss Weston." One Sunday he brought the news that he was going away to sea. It was his last meeting, and the tears were in his eyes as he said good-bye with the words: "Never mind: it is God's will; my Saviour will be with me. And as soon as we come into Plymouth Sound again I shall be up at these dear old meetings like a shot."

And so Arthur went to sea. He was so happy and bright, that, although he was so young, the rough sailors could not help feeling his influence; his little lamp was kept burning so clear that it made a light in a dark place. It shows what influence one who is shining for Jesus may have, that very often a wicked man would stop swearing if he noticed that Arthur was near. The secret of his brightness was his keeping near to Jesus. If you really love any one, you are sure to try to go and be with them when you can. So as Arthur loved his Saviour he wanted to be alone with Him when he could, and yet that cannot be very easy on board a ship; not nearly so easy as it is for you to get away upstairs and have a nice little quiet time by your bedside. But where there's a will there's a way, and so every day, during the dinner hour, Arthur used to run down a ladder into a place called the "bag-racks," that he might be a little while alone with Jesus. I expect it must have been very dark down there, but he would not mind that.

One day he tripped down the ladder as usual. There was an open hatchway just below; perhaps he slipped, perhaps it was too dark to see, we can never know how it was, but he fell, and in an instant Arthur was in glory. No bones broken, no marks on his body, no time for any pain at all!

Was it not beautiful! going happily down to pray to his beloved Lord in the dark, and all at once finding himself in the light of His presence caught away to be with Jesus for ever! It was "sudden death, sudden glory." Would sudden death be sudden glory to you?

A TALK WITH PHILIP THE BOATMAN.

"WELL, I do wish they'd come! Tom and Carrie said they would only be a few minutes after me, and I think they will be all day."

"And I do wish you'd please to sit still, Master Henry," said Philip the boatman. "You jump about like a young sprat. You'd have slipped off the rock half a dozen times if I hadn't had tight hold of you. Loose your hand, and let you catch hold of me instead? No, no, sir! I can't trust *you* to keep hold, you'd soon let go, and then down you'd be into the water!"

"No, I shouldn't!" said Henry. "And if I did you could pull me out, fast enough."

"Daresay I could, Master Henry, but what a mess you'd be in! And then you would have to be sent back to have your wet clothes taken off, and be put to bed instead of coming out for a beautiful sail with me. See what you'd lose if I loosed hold of you. And how should I answer to your papa, when I promised him I'd bring you safe home before dark, and not let you get into any mischief either? No, no, sir, as sure as my name's Philip, I'll keep my word to him! They shan't say that Philip didn't take care of any little gentleman that came along with *him* in his boat."

"I didn't hear you promise that to papa," said Henry.

"Ah, but I did though," said Philip, "before ever I came to fetch you. I'm answerable to him for you. Now if you'll sit quiet I'll tell you what that reminds me of."

Henry was not a great hand at sitting quiet generally, but he was very fond of Philip and liked hearing him talk. It was very pleasant there, with the little waves lapping against the steps in the afternoon sun; and he was very comfortable, perched on the rock, with his little foot resting in the boatman's great strong hand. So as Tom and Carrie were not in sight he thought he could not do better than listen.

"All right, Philip, spin away!" said he.

"Well, Master Henry, seems to me it's this way," began Philip. "The Bible says that God promised eternal life before the world began (Titus 1:2). Now who was there for Him to promise it to? You see He must have promised it to *somebody*, else it wouldn't be a real promise. He didn't promise it to the devils, that's for certain; and He didn't promise it to the angels, else He'd have told us.

And He didn't give the promise to us, because we were not there! Why, Adam himself wasn't made, let alone you and me! Now, Master Henry, who *was* there, for God to give the promise to?"

Henry shook his head; he didn't see it yet. So Philip went on.

"There was One there, Master Henry, before the world began; One that loved us with an everlasting love. Don't you know?"

"Do you mean the Lord Jesus?" said Henry.

"That's it; the Lord Jesus Christ was there, and so God gave Him the promise of eternal life for us; that is, for you, Master Henry, and for me, bless the Lord!" said Philip looking up.

"But I don't see what that's got to do with your keeping hold of my foot," said Henry.

"Don't you see, sir, when God gave the promise of eternal life to the Lord Jesus, for Him to hold for every one that came to Him, the Lord Jesus undertook that they should *have* it, and that He would bring them all safe home to glory. And He undertook that when we *weren't there*, just the same as I undertook to bring you safe back tonight, and told your father I'd be sure and take care of you, when you weren't there and didn't know anything about it?"

"Then that's why you *will* keep hold of me?" said Henry.

"Yes, sir," said Philip, "and that's why the Lord Jesus will keep hold of us, and won't let us be lost. He's undertaken us, and He will answer to the Father for us; and He knows we should be lost if it only depended on our keeping hold of Him. So if we have come to Him and are coming along with Him (just like you have come along with me, Master Henry), we need not ever be afraid of being lost, because it's quite certain He'll do what He undertook, and never loose us. You're not a bit afraid of tumbling over into the water, are you, Master Henry, for all it's rather deep just off the steps?"

Henry laughed. "Afraid! Why I couldn't tumble in, Philip, while you keep such tight hold."

"But if I'd only given you my hand to lay hold of I'll warrant you'd not have kept hold two minutes, and more likely than not you'd have wriggled off the rock into the water in another minute. All the more likely because you wouldn't have had the thought to be afraid! There is the greatest danger when we're *not* afraid, if Jesus hasn't got hold of us. But if He has hold of us we are safe. It says, 'With Me thou shalt be in safeguard.'"

Henry looked very thoughtful. He had forgotten all about Tom and Carrie. It was a good thing they had been so long in coming! At last he said, "I suppose that's the same thing as 'Safe in the arms of Jesus,' that we sing. But how do people know when Jesus has got hold of them?"

Philip was quite sharp enough to guess that when Henry said "people" he really meant himself; and that he would like to know whether the Lord Jesus had hold of him, only he was too shy to put it in that way.

So Philip answered: "See here, Master Henry, how do you know I'm answerable for you, and taking care of you? Wasn't the first thing in it just that you came along with me, when I told you the boat was waiting, and that your papa told me I might come and fetch you? And then, *after you had come*, I told you (didn't I?) that I had promised him I'd take care of you and bring you safe back! And then, you see, here you are along with me, and talking with me; and there's no doubt at all about that! Now it's just the same with *Him*. He has asked you to come along with Him. He has called out loud to you, 'Come unto Me!' till you know the words as well as your own name. And as sure as ever you take Him at His word and come to Him, and tell Him you'll go along with Him, so sure He'll *take* you along with Him, and keep tight hold of you and not let you be lost. Why, He's *told* you so in ever so many texts, and He always tells true. And then, after that, He'll explain things to you by His Holy Spirit; you'll be surprised what beautiful things He'll explain to you! And then you'll be talking with Him, and finding out for certain what a Friend you've got. And one verse I know will look as if it was written all in sunshine for you, 'My sheep shall *never* perish, *neither shall any man pluck them out of My hand.*' I am glad He's told us that."

> All that the Father gave
> His glory shall behold;
> Not one whom Jesus came to save
> Is missing from His fold.
>
> He shall confess His own
> From every clime and coast,
> Before His Father's glorious throne,
> Before the angel host.
>
> "O righteous Father, see,
> In spotless robes arrayed,
> Thy chosen gifts of love to Me,
> Before the worlds were made.
>
> • • • • •
>
> "As Thou hast lovèd Me,
> So hast Thou lovèd them;
> Thy precious jewels they shall be,
> My glorious diadem!"

THE SPIRIT OF BEAUTY.

THE Spirit of Beauty had wandered through the world from the first dawn of creation's morning. Man was subject to her, but he knew her not. Glimpses of her ethereal form gladdened him; but as yet she dwelt in his earth as a veiled virgin, and none had seen her countenance, only the reflection of her smile.

Then the Spirit of Beauty sighed, and said: "Man is my vassal; he acknowledges me as a power mysterious and superior, but he hath not beheld me; and how then shall he fully know and love me? Who shall reveal me to him? Where shall I find one who may undertake the mighty task?"

For the Spirit loved the soul of man, and longed to rejoice him with a revelation of her ineffable loveliness. So she went forth and walked through the world, to find one worthy to be the vehicle of her manifestation; and, lo, a fair young girl sat by a fountain, her head bent in quiet musing; and the Spirit loved her, and said, "Even she shall become the revealer of my power to the hearts of men." And from the sparkling waters the Spirit of Beauty, ascending, entered into her spirit, and looked forth from her brow, till men wondered and said, "Surely the Spirit of the Beautiful is among us"; and they worshipped before her. Then the heart of the maiden was lifted up with pride, and an unholy light was mingled with the rays which the fair Spirit had poured from her starry eyes, and the purity was gone. So the Spirit was grieved, and said, "I cannot dwell with one who harbours the fell child of him who disturbed the harmony of my home, even heaven." And she sped away to seek a more perfect resting place, leaving but a trace of her bright presence, like the quivering light of the summer sky at midnight.

Then the Spirit saw one who thought to perpetuate his name by a monument which should stand when the oak sapling at his door had become the riven and hollow trunk of a thousand winters. She overshadowed him with her influence as with an invisible mantle; and, under his master hand and eye, there arose a fair temple, whose arching roof and carven pillars should be the interpretation of the mighty Spirit. "Shall he not reveal me to man?" said she; and awhile she paused, resting in the thought. But Superstition crept, with serpent stealthiness, through the fane,[1] leaving her defiling trail upon pavement and

---

[1] fane: temple.

dome, and before that child of Darkness, she, Light's eldest daughter, fled in dismay.

Again she wandered on, roaming over lake and mountain, river and valley, gilding all with a touch of her sun-tipped wand; and the few who met her bowed before her, and acknowledged her veiled presence.

At length she found one leaning upon a broken and tuneless harp, whose remaining strings trembled and wailed in the fitful breeze. She breathed upon it, and it was once more new, and every chord rang forth an echo of her own sweet voice. "Thou shalt reveal me to mankind," said the Spirit; "thy song shall be my incarnation." And the harpist went forth among men in the fulness of his inspiration, pouring forth melody like rivers of stars and diamonds. His song entered into the hearts of men, and drew out the hidden music of their spirits in response; and they wept, and said, "Thou art mighty, O Spirit, that dwellest in the deep ocean of melody, and ridest on its gushing waves!" But the Spirit was sad, for she was not truly revealed; it was only a single beam of her loveliness glistening through her unraised veil, and as yet men knew her not.

Again she passed through the world on her yet unfulfilled errand, each print of her ruby foot marked with upspringing blossoms; her voice echoed in the carols of myriads of joyous birds, winged forest flowers. On she hastened, until the dingy walls of a busy city rose gloomily before her. Amid its turmoil dwelt one having little in common with the heaving pulses of its restless heart, one who loved and sought the mysterious Spirit of Beauty, and strove to enchain her ethereal essence with the glowing fetters which his skilful pencil forged. Already had he revealed, not the Spirit herself, but the dream of her image which had arisen in his soul. Others were satisfied, and deemed that he had found her; but there was a craving within him which spoke out loud and strong: "Onward! thou hast not found the reality of thine ideal!" And the Spirit of Beauty pitied him, and said, while she laid her rainbow hand upon him, "Through thy bright creations shall men behold and love me." And his beautiful imaginings became yet more beautiful; his canvas glowed with tints more fairy-like and tender; he rejoiced in the new powers with which he had been endowed, and adored the lovely children of his thought. "Thou art revealed, O Spirit of Beauty!" was his triumphant cry. But the Spirit sighed, for she knew that it was not so. The shadow of earth rested upon his work, dimming his brightest hues, beclouding his fairest forms, and men still gazed upon the unlifted veil.

Then came Night in her silent-wheeled and ebon chariot, tracking her starlit course. In her hand she bore slumberous poppy garlands to entwine many a brow where anxious thought held tumultuous sway through the long weary daylight; and the Spirit of Beauty kissed her, till her countenance grew fair even in its swarthy gloom, and a coronet of stars shone forth among her raven tresses. Beneath them wandered alone, holding strange wild converse with himself, one who shunned men, and their hateful and hating ways. And the Spirit spoke: "To him, O Night, send not thy poppy wreath, till thy journey of blessing is well-nigh ended; let his be the last which thou shalt twine, for I would speak with him beneath the shadow of thy chariot." And she descended upon him on the wing of a soft moonbeam, and said: "Many have failed me, yet once more will I seek a revealer; to thee I come as worthy of the task." Then wonderful thoughts arose in giant beauty from the depths of his soul, and bright images flashed athwart the dark abysses of his spirit, his eye was lit by an inward flame, and his cheek flushed like the crimson cloud of sunset; and he knew that he ranked with the master-spirits of the world. From a lava fount of poetic fervour rose burning and sparkling thoughts, ever changing, ever new, blending in their ardent radiancy, till as a tide of lofty verse they burst from his unsealed lips. Fancy soared at his bidding throughout the realms of the Known, ever and anon with bolder flight invading the confines of the Unknown, returning laden with its wealth of beauty to lay at his feet. His words echoed among the nations; the world, his entranced auditory, stood still to listen and admire; the magic sway of his mighty genius universal submission recognised.

But alas! a spring of earthly passion welled up in his heart, mingling with the fountain of thought which the Spirit of Beauty had created within him; the fire-glancing splendour of its leaping billows was darkened and sullied by its dusky flow; and even from its most shining waves her image faded in gloom, for they too were defiled.

Then the Spirit wept, and said: "I will return to the home where I dwelt ere the grim rule of Chaos passed away from earth. In the eternal light of heaven I may rest in unveiled loveliness, amid the holy and blessed ones who know and love me, as men, with all their forced ecstasies and fancied raptures, never may." And as she wept, her tears fell into the ocean depths, and became hidden yet shining pearls, while in a chariot of lightning she prepared to depart. But while her foot yet clung with lingering desire to the soil she was stayed from her swift ascent. For One stood beside her whose presence chained her as with a sovereign spell, and she bent and kissed the ground on which He trod. He knew what it was to wander through the world unknown, even as she had done; but He was not only unknown, but unloved, yea more, despised and rejected. Sorrow had walked beside Him on His weary way, and grief had been His daily companion. To His own He came, and they received Him not, hiding their faces from Him, and deeming that He had no beauty that they should desire Him. Then the Spirit of Beauty gazed upon the grave yet winning majesty of

His countenance, and said: "My wanderings shall cease, for Thou shalt reveal me! In Thee alone may the sons of men behold the perfect beauty for which they have groped in vain since the hand of Adam wove the twilight veil which hides me from their sight." And while she gazed, behold, the veil was lifted, and she stood revealed in the fulness of her radiant loveliness.

With Him she went forth again through the dark wastes of the earth, shining in every glance of His eye, whispering in the music of His words; and men knew and loved her, seen in the light of the altogether Lovely One. And though there were still many who saw her not, because they lifted not their eyes to gaze on Him who alone might manifest her, yet she forsook not their now brightened dwelling; waiting till, amid the glories of a great and surely coming day, HE, THE ONLY REVEALER OF BEAUTY, should be the desire of every eye and the joy of every heart.

TO F. R. H.'S BRUEY BRANCH.

The Mumbles, Swansea,
April 2nd, 1879.

My dear Collectors:

God has given us one of the most splendid answers to prayer I ever knew. He has prospered your Bruey branch ever so much beyond what *I* asked or thought, and so maybe it is beyond what you asked or thought either! So those of us who have been faithfully remembering to pray for our work on Monday mornings may have the joy of hearty thanksgiving for answered prayer; and if those who have been forgetting all about it will nevertheless join in thanking Him for doing what they did *not* ask, I think they will be glad to join in our prayer after this!

Two years ago we started with eight collectors, and sent up £20 9s. 1d.

Last year we had eighteen collectors, and sent up £41 9s. 3d.; and this year we have eighty-six collectors, and have sent up £108 19s. 1d. Is not this grand! And this is not nearly all. Mr. Roe, one of the association secretaries, tells me that he has "hundreds of cards out, and is appointing twig secretaries in all directions." So that dear little Bruey's work is bearing most wonderful fruit, and it looks as if there would be a great deal more next year than this. We have five twigs in the Bruey branch, besides the senior and junior divisions; but it seems we shall have a *great* many more soon.

Now as our faithful God has heard our poor little prayers so far, I want you to pray still more, and especially that He would not only help us in our collecting, but that He would send a very great spiritual blessing on the work done in Ireland by means of the money collected. Will you join me in asking four things?

1. That God would give His Holy Spirit to all the Irish teachers and their pupils.

2. That very many may during this year seek and find Jesus.

3. That those who find Him may be filled with love, and that the joy of the Lord may be their strength, especially in bearing persecution for His sake.

4. That every one who finds Christ may begin at once to bring others to Him.

I wish you would just copy these four things out, and put them in your Bibles, so that you may be reminded every Monday morning *what* to pray for. And we shall see what gracious answers God will give us. "The Lord *hath* done great things for us," and it seems as if He were saying, "thou shalt see greater things than these"; so "be glad and rejoice, for the Lord *will* do great things." Find these three texts out, and mark them in your Bibles.

Now for some business remarks. I wish you would all learn to be business like! Some of you did everything right, and I herewith offer my best thanks, as secretary, for their having saved me a good deal of trouble by doing *all* I asked. But why did so many of you forget to make your P.O.O.'s payable at The Mumbles? Nearly half of you made them out to *Swansea*, which gave me a great deal of extra trouble, as it is six miles off, while The Mumbles is within a walk. Then how was it that I had to write to seven or eight of you because the 1st of March went by and you did not send your card in? Some of you even then kept me waiting, and thus I was defeated in a very nice little plan I had, which I meant to have written to each of you about, to reach you on St. Patrick's Day, March 17th. I will see if I can do it next year! *One* thing nearly everybody was very good about this time, and that was in forwarding the circulars. The senior division circular went round without one single day missed. But I want to explain that I never object to your keeping the circular another day or two, if it is really for a good purpose, if you want to show it to two or three friends who might be interested to see it, or if you are away from home and wanted some one there to see it, and so post it round by them. This is a very different thing from keeping it for nothing.

Only when you do so it would be a good plan if you wrote a word or two on the circular to explain why it was not sent on at once, and then I should know it was not carelessness, and perhaps should have the pleasure of seeing that it was doing a little more work. Just one thing more: now that I have so many collectors, I cannot undertake to recollect their addresses *off hand*, so when you write to me, or to any one else who has a great many letters to write, please always put your *full* address at the top of your letter, and then I have not to stay to hunt it out in my address book.

Do you remember my asking you to pray for a dear little girl? Her mamma writes as follows: "I enclose £5, our darling Nony's collection for the Irish Society, and which in all probability will be her last, as the doctors say she is now past recovery, and that it is only a question of *time*." What an unspeakable comfort and perfect rest it gives us, to feel that our *times* are in His hand whose way is *perfect!* So we cannot for one moment wish anything otherwise than as *He* orders it. The work sold was not *all* her own doing, but she worked a few minutes at a time as long as she was able. She has had two operations during the last month, and has a large wound in her thigh. Her sufferings have been terrible, but I have never heard a murmur. It was so kind of you to ask prayer for her, and seemed to please her much." Please remember, more, poor little Nony,[1] and ask the Good Shepherd to deal very tenderly with His little suffering lamb. Surely He will send a special blessing on *her* work, " the few stitches " done " as long as she was able."

I am sending a copy of the February number of *Day of Days* to each collector. If any one does not receive it, please let me know. I particularly want you *all* to take the little magazine in, and recommend it to your subscribers; it is only a penny a month. For now we have arranged to have something about the Irish work in it every month, so that all collectors and contributors will be able to get fresh accounts, besides a great deal else that will be nice to read. The one I send contains a paper called " Novel kind of Schools." The March number (which I do hope you will get) has one called "*How very Irish!*" April will have—well, you get it and see what!

Next June I hope, please God, to go to Ireland myself, on purpose to go to the parts where our Society is at work, and then I shall write all about what I saw and heard, and have it printed in the magazine, which will be better than these short circulars, and I hope much more interesting. That's another thing I want you to pray for: ask that, if it is God's will I should go and do this, I may be both blessed and made a blessing in doing it.

And now I will give you a text for your next year's work: " Be not weary in well doing." Perhaps some of you *are* a little bit weary in it; some have owned that they are, as they sent up a card not quite so full as last year. One loving elder sister writes of a younger one: " She is very sorry it is less than last year, but somehow the dear child has not been quite so mindful of it this last year, and she is terribly shy of asking strangers. However, I do trust the loving Saviour will lay it on her heart with enduring power, that she may work for Jesus' sake only, and not get weary now the novelty has worn off." That is just what I pray for every one of you dear ones, whether I know you personally or not.

To that loving Saviour I commend you and your work for the coming year.

Your very affectionate Secretary,

FRANCES RIDLEY HAVERGAL.

[1] See " Memorials of Little Nony," by her Mother. London: Nisbet & Co.

CEDAR TREE, WINTERDYNE.

(See pages 6 and 49.)

Cedar Tree at Winterdyne. (*See pages 4 and 25.*)

TRUSTING JESUS.

Words and Music by F. R. HAVERGAL.

I am trust - ing Thee, Lord, Je - sus, Trust - ing on - ly Thee;

Trust - ing Thee for full sal - va - tion, Great and free.

I am trusting Thee for pardon;
 At Thy feet I bow,
For Thy grace and tender mercy,
 Trusting now.

I am trusting Thee to guide me;
 Thou alone shalt lead!
Every day and hour supplying
 All my need.

I am trusting Thee for cleansing
 In the crimson flood;
Trusting Thee to make me holy
 By Thy blood.

I am trusting Thee for power;
 Thine can never fail!
Words which Thou Thyself shalt give me,
 Must prevail.

I am trusting Thee, Lord Jesus:
 Never let me fall!
I am trusting Thee for ever,
 And for all.

The Angels' Song.

Words and Music by F. R. HAVERGAL.

Now let us sing the Angels' Song,
   That rang so sweet and clear,
When heav'nly light and music fell
   On earthly eye and ear.
To Him we sing, our Saviour King,
   Who always deigns to hear:
     "Glory to God! and peace on earth,"
     For evermore. Amen

He came to tell the Father's love,
   His goodness, truth, and grace;
To show the brightness of His smile,
   The glory of His face;
With His own light, so full and bright,
   The shades of death to chase.
     "Glory to God! and peace on earth,"
     For evermore. Amen.

He came to bring the weary ones
   True peace and perfect rest;
To take away the guilt and sin
   Which darkened and distressed;
That great and small might hear His call,
   And all in Him be blessed.
     "Glory to God! and peace on earth,"
     For evermore. Amen.

He came to bring a glorious gift,
   "Goodwill to men;" and why?
Because He loved us, Jesus came
   For us to live and die.
Then, sweet and long, the Angels' Song
   Again we raise on high:
     "Glory to God! and peace on earth,"
     For evermore. Amen.

New Year Hymn.

1.

Jesus, blessèd Saviour,
    Help us now to raise
Songs of glad thanksgiving,
    Songs of holy praise.
O how kind and gracious
    Thou hast always been!
O how many blessings
    Every day has seen!
        Jesus, blessèd Saviour,
            Now our praises hear,
        For Thy grace and favour
            Crowning all the year.

2.

Jesus, holy Saviour,
    Only Thou canst tell
How we often stumbled,
    How we often fell!
All our sins (so many!),
    Saviour, Thou dost know;
In Thy blood most precious,
    Wash us white as snow.
        Jesus, blessèd Saviour,
            Keep us in Thy fear,
        Let Thy grace and favour
            Pardon all the year.

3.

Jesus, loving Saviour,
    Only Thou dost know
All that may befall us
    As we onward go.
So we humbly pray Thee,
    Take us by the hand,
Lead us ever upward
    To the Better Land.
        Jesus, blessèd Saviour,
            Keep us ever near,
        Let Thy grace and favour
            Shield us all the year.

4.

Jesus, precious Saviour,
    Make us all Thine own,
Make us Thine for ever,
    Make us Thine alone.
Let each day, each moment,
    Of this glad New-year,
Be for Jesus only,
    Jesus, Saviour dear.
        Then, O blessèd Saviour,
            Never need we fear,
        For Thy grace and favour
            Crown our bright New-year!

A Prayer.

O God wash me from all my sins in my Saviour's blood, & I shall be whiter than snow. Fill me : with the Holy Ghost for Jesus Christ's sake, Amen.

This prayer was written in an original copy (published by James Nisbet & Co.) of Ben Brightboots, and Other True Stories, Hymns, and Music, *at the end of the book. We do not know who wrote this.* A Prayer. O God wash me from all my sins in my Saviour's blood, and I shall be whiter than snow. Fill me with the Holy Ghost for Jesus Christ's sake, Amen.

Manufactured by Amazon.ca
Acheson, AB

12382555R00050